Let's Do Poetry

in Primary Schools!

James Carter

Published 2012 by A&C Black,
an imprint of Bloomsbury Publishing Plc
50 Bedford Square, London, WC1B 3DP
www.bloomsbury.com

ISBN 978-1-4081-6391-7
Text © James Carter 2012
Design © Marcus Duck
Illustrations © Sam Church/www.organisart.co.uk

A CIP record for this publication is available from the British Library.

Printed and bound in Great Britain by CPI Group (UK) Ltd, Croydon CR0 4YY

10 9 8 7 6 5 4 3 2 1

This book is produced using paper that is made from wood grown in managed, sustainable forests. It is natural, renewable and recyclable. The logging and manufacturing processes conform to the environmental regulations of the country of origin.
To see our full range of titles visit **www.bloomsbury.com**

Acknowledgements

All poems are copyright © the authors and have been included by kind permission of the copyright holders. Grateful acknowledgement is made to the publishers of the following publications in which poems previously appeared.

All efforts have been made to seek permission for copyright material, but in the event of omissions, the publisher would be pleased to hear from the copyright holders and to amend these acknowledgements in subsequent editions.

Poems by James Carter first published in the following titles: 'Night Car Journey' from Cars, Stars, Electric Guitars (Walker Books); 'Tree', 'Take A Poem', 'Night Soup', 'Words', 'Love You More' from Time-travelling Underpants (Macmillan Children's Books); 'Happy Poem', 'Where Did We Go?', 'Pirate Pete', 'Splish! Splash! Splosh!' from Hey, Little Bug! (Frances Lincoln): 'What Stars Are', 'This is Where…', 'If' from Journey to the Centre of My Brain (Macmillan Children's Books); 'Haiku'. 'Tiger Haiku', 'Hare & Tortoise Senryu', 'Tanka: Monkey', 'Cinquain: Sealions', 'What To Say If You Meet A Ghost', 'Little Alien!', 'Zim Zam Zoom!', 'Saturn!' (with Madeleine Carter), 'WALT and WILF', 'The Ancient Greeks', 'The Story of Water', 'Night Cat', 'Porky Pies!' all published here for the first time, copyright © James Carter 2012. Extracts of poems by James Carter first published in the following titles: 'Happy Poem', 'It's Where', 'Crayon Poem', 'Bears, Bears, Bears', 'Caterpillar' from Hey, Little Bug! (Frances Lincoln); 'Love You More', 'World of Weird' from Time-travelling Underpants (Macmillan Children's Books); 'The Dark' from Cars, Stars, Electric Guitars (Walker Books); 'FISH!', 'Little Alien!', 'Wild, Wild Weather', 'Bucket!' all published here for the first time, copyright © James Carter 2012.

'The Listeners' by Walter de la Mare (published 1912); 'Heaven' by Brian Moses from Holding the Hands of Angels published by Salt Publishing (2011); 'Playgrounds' by Berlie Doherty from Walking On Air published by Hodder Children's Books (1999) ; 'The Corn Scratch Kwa Kwa Hen and the Fox' by Julie Holder from My First Book of Oxford Book of Animal Poems published by OUP (2005) .

Children's poems: 'Poppy Limerick' by Madeleine Carter, South Moreton Primary School; 'Munch Crunch Munch!' extract by Laura, Year 2 class, St John's Infants, Newbury; 'How Do Animals Feel?' by Year 1 classes of All Saints CE Primary School, Didcot; 'Anatomical Rap' by Year 4 class, Telferscot Primary School, London; 'What Was I?' by the Infant class at Dorchester St Birinus CE Primary School, Dorchester-On-Thames; 'The Queen' by Harry Salmon, Year 4, Leehurst Swan School, Salisbury; 'The Black Hole' by Sithara Gunarajah, Year 6, South Moreton Primary School; 'Dragon's Cave' by Finn Walshe Year 5, South Moreton Primary School; 'To Grandad' by Ryan Walshaw, Year 6, Rise Park Junior School; 'To My Family' by Cordelia Dyter-Lyford, Year 7, St Paul's Catholic College; 'Moonlit Gathering' by Abigail Plant, Lake Middle School, IOW; 'Let's go by…' by Year 1 & 2 classes, Kintbury St Mary's CE Primary School, West Berkshire; 'RAINFOREST' Acrostic by Lily Philips, Falklands Primary School

Contents

Introduction

How poetry can enrich, engage and inspire

Imagine this: once a year a teacher brings out a box of musical instruments – guitars, violins, keyboards, percussion, harps, drums, all kinds. The children are allowed to play them all – but only for two weeks. The children love playing the variety of instruments, and relish the opportunity of being creative and expressing themselves, and even performing to others. The instruments are then put away, back in the cupboard for another year. Of course this is a fictional scenario. Many children get opportunities to play music every week, and they get to grow and blossom as musicians. But unfortunately, this is exactly what happens with poetry in many Primary schools across the UK – poetry is wheeled out as a once-a-year module.

A school that regularly celebrates poetry will be giving their children vibrant, language-rich opportunities to help them become confident, competent and coherent communicators – in reading, writing, speaking and listening. Certainly, poetry is not the only route to achieving this, but why miss out on this exciting and vital resource, this dynamic medium that is so fun and accessible, that children so readily respond to?

Why do children so readily respond to poetry? Well, from what I can tell: its uniqueness, brevity and intensity, its simplicity and directness, as well as its playfulness, its repetition and above all, its musicality.

Children love reading, writing, hearing and performing poetry. For me, this is not a theory, it's a simple fact, and something that I've witnessed in probably every single one of the 1000+ Primary schools I have visited all over the UK and abroad in the last ten years. Whether they are consciously aware of it or not, children love words and the magic and the music that happens when you weave words together. As many have commented before, children are born poets: they innately, instinctively play with language, the sounds, the textures, the rhythms of words, and it's an inherent part of their process of discovery.

And yet, there are few Primary schools that really give poetry any regular attention. Certainly a great many individual classes fully celebrate poetry, but why not whole schools? I believe this may be for many reasons. One of the reasons may be because poetry hasn't been centre stage in any official government strategy, curriculum or assessment procedure. Until recently, poetry has been deemed to be a 'literacy' (that awful, bland, lacklustre word) activity that should be approached in annual modules. This is where '**Let's Do…!**' steps in to provide a comprehensive manual on using poetry as both a creative filter and a foundation for learning, discovery and expression. And, if you don't like the word 'poetry', simply think of it as 'language'.

Common reasons for poetry reluctance

What is evident is that many practitioners have a reluctance to do poetry in any great depth or with any regularity. So often I'm welcomed by a teacher in a school with the phrase, 'Thank you for coming. It's a good thing you're here because we haven't done any poetry for ages.' And here are other prevalent phrases teachers use:

'I don't have time.'

Not enough time? One class I visited in Woking, Surrey has a regular slot every morning – yes, every single morning – in which a child in turn will choose and read a poem out loud to the class. How long does that take? Barely two minutes. And every day. Wow. And children choosing the poems? How democratic. And think of all that wonderful language those children are hearing and absorbing. Every single day. Is that not worth making time for? Has anyone ever said you are not allowed to do that?

'It's not proper writing, like prose.'
'I don't understand poetry.'

Why do so many teachers that I meet confess to preferring teaching prose fiction to poetry? Well, perhaps they feel more comfortable with it. Is prose simpler and more straightforward than poetry? Some teachers are put off by the fact that poetry has so many forms, that they do not know them all, and the rules/structures that each of them has. However, working within these structures for many children can be a rewarding, creative challenge. I would

argue that the conventions of the poetry we give to Primary children are in many ways simpler, more explicit and easier to grasp than prose, and children recognise this themselves. But I'm not here to create a feud between the two as I like them both equally!

'It's scary!'

'Why scary?' I ask. Because, I am told, teachers don't have the confidence, or, more to the point, the training and subject knowledge. Okay, so again that's where **'Let's Do...!'** comes in. The aim of this book is not to turn every teacher that picks it up into a verse-loving, poetry-quoting, sonnet-writing convert – not even to make anyone like poetry. The concept behind **'Let's Do...!'** is simple. It's a resource book, full of practical, fun and meaningful ways of celebrating language in the classroom, across Foundation, and through KS1 and KS2. The idea of this book is to demonstrate that poetry is not the difficult, obscure or academic specialism that many deem it to be. This book provides you with:

- a wide range of materials and resources that will help you to integrate poetry into topic work and activities across the curriculum

- a great many fun, relevant and creative activities that can be put into instant use in the classroom

- guidance on developing a whole-school poetry policy, to show how poetry could, no, *should*, be at the heart of the entire school curriculum

- six or so poetic forms with which to create language-rich and expressive responses to all the topic and curricular work that you cover in the academic year (and there are many more than six here to choose from).

Poetry as a tool for literacy

Poetry is a perfect foundation for a life of literature and language. What is clear as I visit school after school is that many teachers seem unaware that time spent working with poetry will help children to develop not just their poetry-writing skills, but also their prose-writing skills, as well as all of their essential literacy skills. Equally importantly, it develops their confidence and creativity. Poetry is intensive, concentrated language – language with the brightness turned up, and because of this, children will implicitly gain so much knowledge about the way language works: be it, repetition, rhythm, rhyme, alliteration, assonance – as well as metaphor, imagery, narrative, structure and much more. A poem is a microcosm through which to experience language as a whole.

From a pedagogic point of view, poetry is a gift for teachers. Because poetry is something that children innately enjoy, you do not need to work at winning over your classes. For Primary schools, poetry is a wholly flexible,

fun and dynamic medium by which to creatively explore cross-curricular classroom topics: from pirates to Tudors, from Victorians to Ancient Egyptians, from water to islands to time-travel to space and beyond.

To be effective, you need to do poetry regularly (but keep doing those modules/ poetry weeks too), and to bring yourself and your creatives to it. Which teacher guideline told one teacher I met to put on a tracksuit and baseball cap back to front to do raps in the hall with her class? Which guideline told the school I visited in Spain to do Harry Potter kennings? Which directive told one school to have a poetry week, with nearly every activity in every class based around poems?

Sometimes I worry that poetry can be over-analysed at times, even in Primary schools. A pointless, soulless adverb-spotting style exercise will do nothing but switch off those young readers and writers, hence I felt compelled to write this poem.

How To Read A Poem

Search out all the adjectives.
Count up all the verbs.
Make a list of metaphors.
Analyse each word.

Do not talk of feelings
or what it means to you
or how it's magic movie screen
gives pictures fresh and new.

Do not let it sing its song
or weave its mystic web.
Do not let this rhythmatist
beat deep inside your head.

No. Pin it down. Just stab it dead.
The poem must not breathe.
And don't let children love it.
This is literacy.

If done in a creative way, such as discussing how a poet creates a mood, atmosphere or image, there is no harm in asking children which specific words and phrases achieve this, but to sit there simply counting out the certain parts of speech will only increase antipathy towards poetry. Until the age of 16 I thought I hated poetry as all we ever did was deconstruct it. Then, a new teacher turned up. We did Shakespeare's 'Macbeth' and Larkin's 'Whitsun Weddings' and he asked us what we thought of the language and how we felt about it. Wow, we were allowed to respond! Our voices and opinions mattered! This was radical pedagogy for 1976! That teacher, Quentin Edwards, changed my life, and gently directed me on the path to becoming a poet myself.

Who this book is for

Because Primary covers such a very wide range of ages and therefore abilities and interests and expectations, 'Let's Do...!' has to pitch somewhere in the middle, but overall it communicates predominantly to Key Stages 1 and 2. There are, however, many workshops that Foundation teachers could adapt for their own uses. I am a poet and a workshopper, not a classroom teacher. However, every idea, every workshop contained here has been tried and tested in a Primary classroom.

Whilst this book aims to be relevant and practical for all Primary practitioners it is not exhaustive. It can't provide every single form of poetry, or contain a great many poems to read or perform. What it does aim to achieve is to enable teachers to take an overview, and get a good grasp of what poetry can help teachers achieve – creatively, pedagogically, thematically and specifically – with regards to switching on those young readers, writers, thinkers, speakers, listeners and performers.

It did cross my mind as to whether I should indicate which poems and forms are suitable for specific year groups, but that seems too prescriptive to me. A teacher will instinctively know what their classes are capable of/would respond well to.

Finally, on a serious note, 'Let's Do...!' believes that every child should leave Primary school knowing a minimum of ten poems off by heart – poems of all forms and voices and tones – poems that they will take to Secondary school and beyond – poems that will give them rich vocabulary – as well as internal structures, rhythms and cadences to help them to create their own musical and memorable language throughout their lives. How simple and achievable is that?

○

A very brief but huge thank-you to the children and teachers at all the 1000 plus Primary schools I have visited over the last ten years. Thank you for making me feel so very welcome. A few special thank-yous: first to all the teachers and parents of pupils whose wonderful poems feature in this book; also to Debbie Prentice at Falkland Primary School in Newbury and Tina Norton at Kintbury St Mary's CE Primary School for their warm support and encouragement and for allowing me to reflect on residencies in their schools. Finally, thank you to Helen Diamond and Jennifer Carruth for guiding me through the writing of this book.

For all the former staff and pupils of the much loved and never forgotten Highlands School, Reading, 1929-2011

Section One - Poetry in your classroom

Let's Think Poetry

What is a poem?

A box of words – Easy as that! Poems for children are not complex things or overly clever, they are usually simple but well-crafted, and they seek to make a direct communication with their readers.

A spoken song – Song? Yes. Poems are the most musical of all written language forms. Poems have rhythms, rhymes, alliteration, all kinds, to make them more catchy, more memorable, immediate, and are therefore easier to remember and recite.

'A fresh look and a fresh listen' – This is what the poet Robert Frost said, and it's true. The job of a poem is to give you a new way of looking at something and it does this in part by using language in a fresh and exciting way. So, to sum up, the job of a poem it is to say something new.

Language at its most playful – Read a handful of poems and you will find the poet playing around with the sounds and the meanings of words. Poets invent words, use wordplay, puns and twist the meanings of words. Young children are natural poets: they do not know the rules so they play with language however they wish.

Music and meaning – Fundamentally, poems operate on two levels: a) the music, i.e. the language itself, the words, the phrasing, how the poem is laid out and b) the meaning – what the poem is actually about – its theme, its message, its story, its point.

Repetition, repetition, repetition – So many people think that all poems rhyme. Not true! Poems come in all shapes and sizes, from shape poems to raps to limericks, but all of them will have some form of **repetition**. It's what gives poems their music, their catchiness, their shape and their structure.

The most fun you can have with language – What other form of language is ideal for reading, writing, discussing, sharing and performing?

What's so good about poetry? (For teachers)

Most children's poems are **short**, bite-size chunks of text, perfect for regular language activities. Many children that generally struggle with literacy often enjoy poetry because there is less text on the page, and a poem seems more achievable to them.

What's So good about poetry? (For young poets)

It can tell you something you've never heard or thought about before.

It can show you something you've seen before but in a brand new way.

It can stop you in your tracks and make you reflect on something.

It can help you to explore your thoughts, emotions and feelings.

It can show you how other people feel, and how they are like you.

It can show the world in micro as well as the world at large.

It can say a lot in a little – for less is always more in a poem.

It can ask a question or give you an answer.

It can make you laugh, giggle, chuckle.

It can show you how fun, musical and magical words can be.

It can show you something totally amazing.

It can tell you a joke.

It can share a memory with you.

It can entertain you.

It can surprise you.

It can open your mind.

It can be learnt off by heart and carried around in your head forever!

Many children appreciate the **brevity** and immediacy of poems – a little cluster of words can be much less threatening and far more inviting than the seemingly infinite pages of text in a novel.

Poems highlight the **musicality** and **playfulness** of language. Children of all ages relish this aspect of poetry – its rhythms, its cadences, its repetition, its rhyme, its humour, its emotions, its narratives, its ability to let's-look-at-the-world-like-this.

A poem is like a **spoken song**, just waiting to be performed or chanted out loud and brought to life.

Poems are mainly short and punchy, perfect for **learning** and **performing** in assemblies and concerts.

Poetry unites the school as a **community**. Every class from Foundation to Year 6 can participate in poetry events, poetry assemblies, poetry weeks. The whole school can celebrate language together.

Poetry is simply an umbrella term for **many forms** (free verse, acrostics, raps, kennings, shape poems, rhyming couplets etc.) and many of these are suitable for Primary-aged children to explore the many structures, patterns, voices and modes that language can be.

Poems can have a range of **moods** and **tones** – from the lightweight, fun and frivolous to the more profound, thoughtful and spiritual. And, yes, children do clearly enjoy funny poems but they also love the quieter ones too,

the ones that highlight inner realities and emotions.

Poems are ideal for **displays** and **publishing**. Cover your classroom and your school in poems. Put them down every corridor, even in the loos. Put up shape poem displays. Do a 'What's the story?' narrative poem display. Fill a sheet with haikus. Cut the verses up and do a trail down the corridor. Have a poetry section on your school website.

Poetry is one the best **literary forms** for children to write themselves. The very best poetry is often simple and direct – and children can achieve this themselves. What's more, it's the perfect medium for children to write about their own thoughts, emotions, memories and experiences, for making sense of their worlds and the world at large.

Time spent working on poetry is never a waste – for it will enrich, nurture and also help to develop children's **prose** (including **fiction**) **writing skills** and also help to encourage their life-long love of language.

Poems can be written **anywhere** – in the classroom, the playground, on school trips – at farms, art galleries, museums and even during school residential trips.

Children do not take too easily to **drafting** and **editing**. They want to do and complete something within a short time frame. With poetry, you can show children the effect that a couple of minor changes can have on the impact and success of a piece of writing.

Let's Live Poetry

24/7 poetry

Here are some ways you can make poetry a staple in your classroom:

Poem of the day

Some schools have a 'Poem of the day' every single day of the school year. Your class could too, and there are many ways of going about it and it only takes a couple of minutes. As a rule of thumb, it is probably best to pick short, snappy poems, no longer than a page or so. Having said that, a longer one such as Alfred Noyes' 'The Highway Man' or one of Roald Dahl's 'Revolting Rhymes' would go down well too.

Children choose – Over one month, every child in the class picks the poem of the day. It might be a poem from a book at home, or something they spotted in the library. The teacher could ask children to look through all the poetry books in the classroom or school library and pick one. If they wish, each child can read their chosen poem, or ask the teacher to read it to the class.

Teacher chooses – For one month, the teacher can pick a good range of poems, on all kinds of subjects, and even include some of their own favourites.

Topic chooses – For one month, the teacher/children read out poems that explore their current class topic.

Season chooses – For one month, the class read out summer/autumn/winter/spring poems.

PSHE chooses – For one month, the teacher selects a range of poems on topics such as family, friendships, bullying, the world at large, feelings, healthy eating.

Favourite poem – At the end of the week, the class can vote for their favourite poem of that week, and it can be read again at the end of the school day on Friday.

Performance – If the class really take to a particular poem, this could be worked up into a performance piece for a future assembly. For all you need to know about performing poetry, see LET'S PERFORM POETRY p26.

Poet of the month

Each month, have a permanent display featuring copies of a variety of poems by a chosen poet (see LET'S RECOMMEND p126). This could be a modern or classic poet, a poet that the children have met/will meet, a poet-in-residence, a favourite poet of the class or the teacher, a poet that writes on the class topic, a poet that writes shape poems/funny poems/narrative poems/rhyming poems, a poet that the class can have a correspondence with by email or via a website. The poems on the display could be read, discussed or performed in assemblies (see LET'S PERFORM POETRY p26).

The poetry classroom

Here are some ways you can promote poetry in your classroom environment:

Displays – Have a display of poems, with a theme for a month. Say one month features the poems of Benjamin Zephaniah, the next month, Carol Ann Duffy, the following month, John Agard. Another month might be free verse poems by various poets (perhaps Michael Rosen,

Brian Moses, ee cummings), another month shape poems, another month Japanese haiku poems. Have another display for poems of the day or poems of the week written/chosen by children.

Topic displays – Every classroom has specific boards for topic displays. Perhaps one of these could be kept for poems written about the topic, such as Ancient Egyptian kennings, minibeasts acrostics or skeleton raps.

Poetry box – Organise a box in a prominent part of the classroom that is full of poetry books that the children can select and read at given times during the school day.

Picture books – Even well into KS2, children enjoy rhyming picture books. Needless to say, anything by Allan Ahlberg, Tony Mitton, Michael Rosen and Julia Donaldson are well worth keeping in the classroom. Why not get pairs of children in KS2 to rehearse readings of rhyming picture books to EY/KS1?

Poetry posters – These can be obtained from the Education Department of The Poetry Society, 22 Betterton Street, London WC2H 9BX: www.poetrysociety. org.uk. Try also The Poetry Library, based at The South Bank Centre in London: www.poetrylibrary.org.uk

Poetry CDs/DVDs/MP3s – Many poets have made recordings of their work, and have these available on their websites. Try also the fabulous Poetry Archive online: www.poetryarchive.org

Poets' corner – Arrange a desk, beanbag or some place where children can go to write or read a poem, jot down ideas, choose a poem from an anthology.

Poetry ideas notebooks – In some classes, children keep their notebooks in the middle of the table at all times in case they get ideas for their writing. Ideas occur at all kinds of unexpected times – as all writers will tell you – and you have to have a notebook handy to jot them down in.

Poetry folders – These are great for storing all the poetry work that you do throughout the term: poems you write, or copies of poems you read out in class or perform in assemblies.

Poetry section in the school library – Most schools have a great range of poetry books in their libraries – books new or old, on a range of topics and by a variety of poets. Go and check the state of your poetry section. Ask the children to help you and ask what they think about the selection of books.

Where can I find good poetry books?

Here are some places to go to invigorate or replenish your supply of classroom poetry:

Pop into your local library – Go to the children's section and grab an armful of children's poetry books. Take them home. Spend time dipping in and out of them.

Bookshops – Some stock very little poetry at all, whereas others have a truly inspiring selection of poetry titles. Any bookshop will be more than happy to order specific titles for you.

Poets' own websites – Most contemporary poets have their own websites nowadays, which often feature a number of their most popular poems.

So why not pick a poet, find their website, and read, share and discuss some of their poems? There might even be audio/video recordings of the poems on the site. If the class enjoy them, why not write an email to the poet with some positive feedback?

Search online – You'd be amazed at the number of poetry books for sale at sites like Amazon for £0.01! Take a risk. Buy a few. Maybe read the reviews first. Or why not review a poetry book as a part of a literacy lesson? Look online to see what new books are available, or have a look at the back of this book for ideas (see LET'S RECOMMEND p126).

Poetry database – Build up a database of poems for all teachers in your school to use. Keep it on the school intranet or in a folder in the staffroom. You might want to categorise the poems according to age/topics/PSHE/assemblies/special occasions/poetry and book weeks etc.

Charity shops – These wonderful places are treasure troves for great books, and are a nice place to visit on Saturday afternoons.

Share the task – Take a whole bunch of poetry books to an informal meeting in the staffroom. Ask every teacher to pick at least five poems they like, appropriate for the age of their class. Then share them around.

Publishing children's poems

Publishing means so much to children, and gives a point, a purpose, an end product as well as an audience to their writing. Children even relish having their ideas put up on the board during a writing workshop, so just imagine how they feel about having a piece of their own writing represented in some form of publication.

Publishing is much simpler and less time-consuming than it sounds. It can take place on a regular basis, and can take many forms. You could have regular displays – in classrooms, corridors, the school hall. It could be an individual poem by one child, or a group of poems in a set style or on one topic. You could have a 'Poem of the week' by different children, to praise, encourage and motivate different writers. This poem could be read out in the headteacher's assembly. Each class could regularly make a book, an anthology of the children's best poems from one term, or from one class topic. The school website is also perfect for regular publishing. Looking beyond the school, teachers could try local newspapers and radio, as well as poetry podcasts of the children reading their own poems.

Arguably, the most rewarding form of publishing is when children have their poems published in actual books – but beware of organisations out to squeeze hundreds of poems onto one page and take a large fee from parents for doing so. Yet, having said this, a number of teachers and parents have informed me that children can and do gain confidence and an increase in self-esteem by being published in this way. An alternative is for the school to publish a book, and one organisation (please google to find others as well) that does this is www.thelittlebooks.co.uk. The presentation is good, and you can include children's own illustrations.

Section Two - Reading and enjoying poetry

Let's Learn Poetry (the basics)

The ingredients of a poem

Gradually, from Year 1 onwards, children should start to know about the various features of a poem, as it will help them with their reading, performing, writing and reading of poetry, and ultimately give them the tools to create poems of their own. If nothing else, children need to know that in a poem, the most fundamental ingredient is **repetition** – from repetition of words, phrases, lines, verses, syllables, vowels, and consonants. Repetition creates rhythm, rhyme, alliteration, assonance and so on.

Here are the features of a poem that are useful for discussions in class:

Title – How important is a title? Very! It's the way in which we enter the world of the poem. A title doesn't have to be long or fancy, but it has to feel right for that poem. Maybe when you are writing each poem, try a few different titles and see which works best.

Words – Compared with prose, poems have very few words, so literally, every single word counts. Every word can affect and alter the poem's feel and rhythm and flow. A poet deliberately chooses those few words because of their sense and their sound, their music and their meaning.

Lines – Prose is divided into sentences and paragraphs, whereas poetry is divided into lines and verses. In rhythmical, rhyming poems the lines are often of similar lengths, and verses can have the same number of lines – but this is not always the case, as with free verse.

Verse/stanza – A verse, also known as a stanza, is made up of lines. Some poems have every verse the same length, others do not.

Structure – This is how the poem is laid out: the sequence and order of the lines and the verses, from the beginning to the middle to the end.

Rhythm – Easy to say, but harder to spell and harder still to explain, rhythm is how a poem sounds when you read it or speak it aloud. The rhythm depends on a number of things, including – the words, the combination of words, the vowels and the consonants, the numbers of syllables and the lengths of the lines. Put simply, rhythm is the feel and flow of the poem.

Alliteration/assonance – These are very similar, and, along with the rhythm, help to create and contribute to the music of the poem. Alliteration is when words have similar sounds at the start: 'when words' and 'similar sounds' are both examples of alliteration. Assonance is when there are the same sounds inside the words: 'green beads' and 'pink mint' are examples.

Syllables – The word 'poem' has two syllables: 'po-em'. The word 'syllable' has three: 'sy-lla-ble'. Clap them. How many syllables are there in your name? Clap them. When writing a poem, reflect on how many syllables there are in each phrase/line you write. In 'magic that glows, magic that grows, magic that glides and groans', each verb has one syllable and that's why it flows. Likewise 'magic that sparkles, magic that spirals, magic that splinters and sprinkles.' works well because each verb has two syllables.

Rhymes – These are when words have the same sound at the end of the lines in a poem:

> It's where mermaids call their home
> It's where pirates used to roam

Half-rhymes – This is when two words nearly rhyme because they have similar sounds:

> First day feeling *funny*
> by the door cling to *Mummy*

Rhyme structure – This is how the rhymes are patterned over the poem.

A rhyming couplet has an AA rhyme structure:

> Why are we so afraid of the dark?
> It doesn't bite and it doesn't bark.

This verse has an ABCB rhyme structure:

> Bucket full of seaweed (A)
> bucket full of sun (B)
> bucket full of memories (C)
> bucket full of fun! (B)

For a more indepth look at rhyming couplets see LET'S WRITE POETRY FOR A REASON: RHYMES, p77.

Images (also known as 'imagery') – These are the pictures that a poem puts in your mind's eye. The more expressive, the more daring the language you use, the clearer and more striking your imagery will be.

Metaphor – This is when the words say that one thing **is** something else: 'the moon is an old copper coin'.

Simile – This is when the words say that one thing is **like** something else: 'beats like the sail of a stormstruck boat'.

Meaning – What does the poem say? Does it tell a story or a joke? Does it make you look at something, think about something? What does it say to you personally, and how does it make you feel?

The forms of poems

The word 'poetry' is an umbrella term for a great many forms. The forms listed here are the most suitable and most commonly used in the Primary years.

Acrostic/alphabet – Poems in which each line begins with a letter from a word; mid-line acrostics feature the letters at some midpoint during a line. Alphabet poems are acrostic poems in which the lines begin with the 26 letters of the alphabet. See LET'S WRITE POETRY FOR A REASON: Acrostics and alphabets on p109.

Calligram poems – Poems that feature words that are made to look like what they mean. Scary BRIGHT and magical are all calligrams. See 'Saturn' on p39.

Conversation poems – Poems told wholly or mainly through dialogue. Harold Monro's 'Overheard on a Saltmarsh' is probably the most well-known. See LET'S WRITE POETRY FOR A REASON: Conversation free verse poems p105.

Diary/letter poems – As the names suggest, a diary poem is a diary entry, and a letter poem (also known as an 'epistolary') is a poem in the form of a letter.

Free verse – Free verse can read a lot like prose, and has a subtle, quiet rhythm. Though it will employ repetition in the form of alliteration, assonance and listing, it will not usually have end-rhymes, that is, rhymes at the end of the lines. Free verse can at times be autobiographical, telling of the poet's experiences, as with much of Michael Rosen's poetry. See the poems 'We Are Learning To... & What I'm Looking For...!' p43 and 'Heaven' p53.

Kennings – Invented by the Vikings, kennings have two words per line, and the second word ends in the 'er' sound, e.g. 'bone-burier' or 'crazy-creature'. A kenning is essentially a metaphor, e.g. 'sofa-scratcher' is another way of saying 'cat'.

Limericks – Popularised by Edward Lear, limericks are humorous, nonsense, five line poems that have an AABBA rhyme scheme:

There once was a panda called Poppy (A)
who was always a little bit sloppy (A)
She sat on her chair (B)
and played with her hair (B)
and spent the day ever so floppy. (A)

Madeleine Carter,
South Moreton Primary School

Lists – There are three main types of list poem. One is a poem that contains a list of things, for example as in Ian McMillan's modern classic 'Ten Things Found in a Wizard's Pocket'. Another is a poem that uses the same word or phrase to open each line or verse, for example:

Happy as a rainbow
happy as a bee
happy as a dolphin
splashing in the sea

The third is a list-repetition poem, which repeats the key word of the piece, for example:

This fish, that fish
fat as well as flat fish
dog and even cat fish
what a lot of fish!

Monologue – These are poems in the voice of a person or character or narrator, for instance:

I, the moon, would like it known
I never follow people home...

Narrative poems – These are poems that tell a story. Traditionally, these were longer, rhyming pieces, but nowadays, many forms from haikus (see Syllabic poems below) to free verse can have narratives. These stories might be fairy tales, fables, myths, legends, invented stories, all kinds. Michael Rosen's 'Chocolate Cake' is a free verse narrative poem. Brian Moses' 'Aliens Stole My Underpants' is a rhyming narrative poem. See also 'Porky Pies!' p61, 'The Corn Scratch Kwa Kwa Hen and the Fox' p46, 'Wild, Wild Weather' p42, 'We Are Learning To... & What I'm Looking For...!' p45 and 'Heaven' p53 for further examples.

Nonsense poems – Well, as the name suggests, these are poems that make no sense!

> In the world of weird
> all the girls wear beards
> and the boys keep bees in their beds...

Also see 'If, If, If...' p49.

Performance poems – These are often fun, upbeat rhyming poems that work very well in performance. See 'Porky Pies!' p61, 'Splish! Splash! Splosh!' p41, 'Where Did We Go?' p43, 'Wild, Wild Weather' p42, 'Take A Poem' p47.

Raps – Raps are simply modern, rhyming poems with a straightforward AABB (rhyming couplet) rhyme scheme with a bit of added attitude! They may well have 'street', colloquial words such as 'yo', 'bling', 'da hood' and 'innit' to name a few.

Perhaps the best and most well-known children's rap is Jack Ousbey's fantastic 'Gran, Can You Rap?' and is highly recommended for poetry concerts. Google or YouTube it! See also 'Porky Pies!' p61.

Rhyming verse – This poetry has end-rhymes, that is, rhymes at the end of each line. See 'Happy Poem' p37 and many others throughout the anthology section.

Riddles – These can be in a variety of forms, and are poems that act as riddles. Both kennings and cinquains are great for these. See 'What Am I? (a kingsize kenning)' p44.

Shapes – This is a poem in the shape of its subject. See 'Tree' p107, 'What To Say If You Meet A Ghost' p108 and 'Little Alien!' p108.

Syllabic poems – Haiku, cinquain, tanka: all these forms have a set syllable count per line. Haiku and tanka, both Japanese forms, traditionally depict the natural world, and portray a specific place and time. Haikus have three lines of 5/7/5 syllables; tankas have two extra lines: 5/7/5/7/7. Cinquains are of American origin and follow a 2/4/6/8/2 pattern. For a more in depth look at these forms, see LET'S WRITE POETRY FOR A REASON: Syllabic poems p90.

Thin poems – These pieces are often short, thin pieces that are centralised on the page, and have short lines, often made up of a single word, for example:

0th Birthday Poem

I
was
born
on my
birthday
in my
birthday
suit
I
was
pinky
and
wrinkly
and
ever
so
cute
and
ever
so
bald
or
so
I've
been
told
'cos
I
don't
recall
being
0
years
old

James Carter

Let's Read Poetry

Reading, sharing and discussing poems

Want your class to engage in vibrant, exciting and meaningful language-focused activities? Time to do poetry then!

Children generally love poems and despite reluctance from a few teachers, children are more than happy to read and share and talk about poems in a meaningful way.

Perhaps you could put the chosen poem(s) onto the interactive white board, so that the poem can be easily viewed/read by the whole class. You can select just a few of the questions as starting points.

Perhaps the first reading could be done by you, the teacher, to model how the poem can be read. Dependent on the year group, a second reading could be by the whole class. A third reading might possibly involve small groups or individuals. Once the class has a feel for the language, tone, mood, voice, subject and music of the poem, here are some key questions to be used:

- Do you like the poem? Why?

- How does the poem make you feel? Why?

- If you read the poem again, would your opinion change?

- What does the poem say?

- Does the poem make sense to you?

- Does the poem have a story or a message? What is it?

- Have you read a poem like this before? How are they similar and different?

- Does the poem remind you say, of anything you have experienced, or another poem or story, and in what way?

Read the poem out loud again.

- Does it work well out loud? Is it a quiet poem to be read silently, or a performance poem to be brought to life?

- How does the poem sound to you?

- Do you have a favourite part of the poem?

- Do you like any particular words or phrases? Why?

- If you speak a language other than English, can you translate some of the poem for the class? How does it sound in the other language?

- Does it have a rhythm? How does it feel?

- Does the poem rhyme or use alliteration?

- Does the poem have a narrator(s)? Whose is the voice of the poem?

- Do you know where the poem is set? How?

- Does the poem use metaphors or similes?

- What pictures or images can you see when reading the poem through?

- Can you think of another title?

- Would you like to write a poem like this?

- Could you write another verse or two for the poem or even your own version?

- Would you recommend the poem to a friend? Why?

Overall, drawing together some of the ideas above, a simple way to think about a poem is by considering the four **Whats**:

WHAT type of poem is it? Is it in a specific form, say a rhyming verse or a haiku or a list poem? Can you recognise the form of poem? How is the poem laid out and structured?

WHAT does the language of the poem do? This can be very much linked to what type of poem it is, but asks you to think about what words there are, how

these are patterned and crafted, and the effect that these words have. Do the words create images, pictures in your mind?

WHAT is the theme of the poem, or what is the poem about? So having thought about what the words are doing, what are they actually saying as a whole? What does the poem tell you, show you, make you think about? Is there a story or a message? Is it a memory or a reflection on something?

WHAT does the poem say to you, as the reader? Do you like it? Or do you like parts of it? How does it make you feel? Would you like to read more poems like this? Would you like to write one like this?

Reading poems as cross-curricular starting points

As this book keeps reminding teachers, a poem is not just for literacy, and ideally not for simply analysing and deconstructing (as that's what Secondary schools will eventually do in preparation for GCSEs). A poem, by its very nature, needs to be seen as a cross-curricular medium, and poetry is at its very best when allowed to celebrate every aspect of the curriculum.

What follows is a range of activities based around poems – writing, art, ICT and other curricular areas.

Writing

- Write another verse or two to a favourite poem or even your own version of a poem. Are there any features – words, phrases, structures – you could borrow for your own poem? You could write on your own or in a pair.

- Write a letter to the character/narrator in the poem.

- Write a diary entry by the character/narrator.

- Re-write the poem in another form – turning a free verse poem into a haiku, a rhyming poem into a shape poem.

- If it's a modern poem, and you enjoy it, why not write to the poet? See if he has a website. Why not ask the poet if he has other poems like this one?

Drawing/painting

This can be done in a number of ways, including:

- asking the children in groups to illustrate each verse, so you produce a series of images for each verse

- asking the children individually to write out the poem on A3 paper and then design it as a poster

- drawing/painting a class mural based on the poem, on paper and then put this onto the classroom door – so visitors literally walk into the poem.

ICT: font-tastic calligrams/shape poems

Ask the children to type up a poem. Allow them to...

experiment
WITH
different
fonts...

- Perhaps use a loud font (or even colour) for the most exciting words, or put each verse in a font (or colour) of its own. A calligram is a word made to look like what it means, as in THIN **WHITE** **LOUD**. Ask the class to improvise some calligram poems as they work on the computer – to experiment, and to see what happens!

- Shape poems work well if you centralise the text and make the lines varying lengths. If you need to add extra details, why not use punctuation like exclamation marks and question marks. See 'Little Alien!' p108.

Design and technology

The possibilities are endless here. Children could try all kinds of inventive things, like:

- making a Jabberwock monster (find the poem 'Jabberwocky' by Lewis Carroll online)

- designing the house of 'The Listeners' (see the poem on p62)

- making the dragon from 'The Dragon Who Ate Our School' (find the poem by Nick Toczek online)

- making a tree and then use lines/phrases from the poem 'Tree' p107

- making an alien based on the poem 'Little Alien!' p108.

Drama

So many poems work well when read out loud, but there is a vast difference between 'reading' (i.e. simply decoding and saying the words) and 'performing', which is actually bringing the poem to life in a performance. A good performance of a poem will have some dramatic elements anyway. For tips on performing, see LET'S PERFORM POETRY on p26.

Why not take a poem you've read and enjoyed and write a mini-play based around it? So, e.g. you could take Jack Ousbey's 'Gran, Can You Rap?' and maybe write a play about what happens when a child goes to visit their rapping gran! Or for something more KS1-based, how about devising a mini-drama about a trip into space, based around 'Zim Zam Zoom!', p38. Imagine the class are space travellers preparing for their journey to the stars. Why not design and make a hat with a rocket for a special assembly?

Music

As poetry is so very musical anyway, instruments have to be used with caution, as they can a) drown out the words and b) easily lose the rhythm. So, to avoid this, music can be used atmospherically, or even to beat out specific words or phrases in a poem. Percussion instruments, from tambourines to shakers and xylophones, are perfect for creating the subtle atmospheres of the wind, a storm, a busy street, space or the sea.

And why not even represent a poem in musical or rhythmical sounds? Once you have made some sounds or patterns of music, record these, and even represent these musical sounds as shapes on a page.

Let's Perform Poetry

What are the benefits of learning a poem off by heart?

It helps to develop your understanding of language, how meaning is made, how words work.

It helps you to appreciate the musicality of poetry.

It helps you to build a repertoire of internal language models.

It helps you to understand the construction of text.

It gives you a language pattern on which to build your own poems, song lyrics, and even poetry's sibling, prose fiction.

All reading ultimately develops your writing skills.

It gives you something to carry with you, wherever you go, something that you may remember throughout your life.

It's enjoyable – reciting, performing and sharing with others.

It helps you to become a more confident reader, performer and public speaker.

Above all, it's fun!

To some, the thought of learning and performing a poem to an audience can seem daunting, but actually it is much easier than it may initially seem. Most children find it very rewarding and take to performing quickly and easily, and the keenest children in such workshops are often those that are not the strongest writers – so this is a good way into poetry for them. This section gives you advice on how to run performance workshops and concerts.

Running a poetry performance workshop

With poetry performances, think about these key areas (these are summarised in the poetry performance checklist on the previous page):

Find a poem

It is essential that you find a poem that the class really responds to, one that works well in performance. This doesn't mean to say that the only poems you should ask children to perform are the upbeat, comic or 'rap' style poems. I've seen Year 6 classes do some fabulous readings of haikus, free verse and all kinds. But, in the main, it will tend to be the rhyming poems, poems with repetition, with colourful and lively language. See the anthology of poems on p37-62 for inspiration.

However, and to an extent, it's not the poem but the performance that makes it. Someone like Stephen Fry could make the Yellow Pages exciting listening! A creative performance is not only in the text, but in the way that the performer brings it off the page and into the ears and minds of the listener. See performance suggestions for specific poems on p33.

> Think: What is so good about this poem? Why have I chosen it? Why do I want people to listen to it? What can I do to make it entertaining, exciting and engaging for others? How can I bring the audience into the poem with me?

What is the poem about?

Does it tell a story? Does it have a theme or message? How would you explain it to someone else? Or is it simply a fun, playful piece that just wants to be brought to life? Ask different groups in the class to discuss what the poem is about and what it tells us, the reader/listener. It might be worthwhile asking the class if they fully understand the piece, and if there are any difficult words or phrases for them.

How can you bring it to life?

It is not simply a question of reading the words. No way! Think of your class as a poetry choir. How much practice does a choir have to do before a song or piece is ready? Heaps! Remember, in the main, children love performing, and school plays usually only come once or twice a year, so poetry performances allow children additional opportunities to get up and bring words to life. Children need to **experience the process** it takes – from the first read-throughs, to the casting of lines/roles, to embellishing with actions/gestures/props/music, through to rehearsals and to a final performance. Classes will need to be kept on track at times, and it will take a lot of concentration and patience and perseverance, but it's so worth it!

Each poem will warrant a different approach, and each poem will have a number of ways that it can be performed, so it is up to the performer(s) to discover and consider the various possibilities and find out what works best for them.

Roles – Giving the right parts to the right children is fundamental. It's good not to give out set roles too quickly, as you may find that some children shine better in some parts than others. (It is worth bearing in mind that teachers tell me that they try and give good parts to those that don't always shine in literacy, to give them a chance to have success in a language-centred activity.)

Essentially, a group of performers, however large or small is like a poetry choir, working together to create a performance for voices. There are four main ways of organising a performance.

First, as a **solo** performance, perhaps even with a 'chorus' coming in for certain parts. Next, poems can be done by a **pair** of children doing various lines or verses each, or coming together for specific parts. Then there is a **small group**, with set lines being undertaken by individuals and/or pairs within the group, then joining together for designated parts or refrains. With a **whole class ensemble** there is scope for all kinds of different permutations. It could be that every child is designated their own lines(s), or pairs/groups are given set lines, or some children are speakers, others act out the poem (with actions/gestures/mimes) or join in for choruses only.

One thing that young performers find hard is switching off when not actively performing, yet still being alert and ready to come in for their next part. As difficult as it can be, children need to remain attentive, and not lose concentration. However, once children know a poem by heart, and they are not reading from sheets they can become more focused, and this is one of a number of reasons why it is vital for children to learn the piece.

Whatever you decide, it is best to go in with some idea before you begin the performance workshop, or otherwise it can get chaotic with various children suggesting different ideas.

Volume – Microphones are ideal, but if there is only one microphone, and there is

a group/whole class, aside from handing the microphone around, it might be best done without. Even when children are whispering or speaking softly, they will need to find ways to project their voices – to be heard at the back of the hall/ performance area.

Pace – Every poem has a rhythm of some kind or another, even free verse. What is hard for children and many performers is to read rhythmical, rhyming poetry without doggedly following the rhythmic pattern like a metronome. This takes much time and practice, but certainly going at a slow (and I mean slow!), steady pace will help – as well as perhaps even pausing occasionally, for emphasis, and to break the rhythmic flow. Music often does this too, and the listener's ear will then anticipate the rhythm commencing again.

Even adults, once the nerves/adrenalin kick in, find it hard to keep performances at an even, steady pace at times. Children need to be regularly told that however slow they think they are going, it will probably not be slow enough. Counting children in at the start of a poem may well help, as well as recording a trial run and listening back and asking the performers if they feel they are going too fast. As a general rule, the slower the delivery the better, even with raps and the more rhythmical poems. If you go too fast the words and their meanings will be lost. And what is the point of a performance if the poem can't be heard? Older children will realise that throughout a poem, you can speed up or slow right down for emphasis, and even take a pause for dramatic effect. This can be done with Upper KS2 classes that have more experience of performing.

Mood – Depending on the poem, this can be quite a subtle thing to grasp. But, the essential question to ask during the rehearsal process is, are the children not just saying the words, but meaning the words, and bringing out the mood, the atmosphere, the tone of the poem? If it's spooky, or thoughtful, or funny or spiritual or reflective, whatever, does the delivery bring this out?

More experienced performers might want to think about pitch and timbre and the tonal quality of the voice. For a scary or spooky voice, children might choose to make their voices deeper, and for emphasis might want to screech out a high sound for the occasional word.

Express – Beyond the words and how they are spoken, many things can bring a poem to life: non-verbals, pauses, actions, gestures, movements, hand claps, foot stomps, costumes, props, eye contact, music, all kinds – but don't overdo it. To an extent, the words should be allowed to do their work, and less is more, and simplicity is often best.

Use of music – The one area I'm sometimes reluctant to promote is music, as more often than not, when children perform a poem with either musical backing or a rhythmical accompaniment, the music either drowns out the voices, or the percussion is counteracting the rhythm of the poem. So what to do? It's a question of moderation and trial and error.

A musical backing in a poetry performance is a great idea, and can work well, with either recorded music or live instruments (from guitars and stringed instruments to pianos to percussion such as glocks and xylophones) – but the instruments must **not** drown out those voices. Two easy solutions might be a) to have the musicians at the back of the stage, the performers at the front (but still close enough to hear each other, and keep in sync) or b) to have the music playing at the very start, before the poem begins, and at the end of the poem, when it has finished. Yet if you want it playing throughout, you will need

to drop the volume right down whilst the voices take over.

As regards percussion, I would actually suggest that unless you have a very talented percussionist – or beatboxer/vocal percussionist – in your class, it is best to do a poem without rhythmical backing. I've seen many Year 5 and 6 classes performing with rhythmical percussion backing that falls apart during the first verse because the rappers/musicians can't keep in time with each other. But, if you are keen to try it, please do prove me wrong here.

However, one form of percussion that I've seen work very well in a number of poetry concerts is what I term chestbone/handclap percussion. It's best done by a whole group or ensemble, and it works like this: think of the drum intro to the Queen song 'We Will Rock You'. If you don't know it, find it on YouTube! The drum part is made up of a) bass drum and b) snare drums/hand claps. (Please note I've simplified the groove slightly here.) For the bass drum part you do a single beat with your open hand gently but firmly on to your chestbone, then a single clap with both hands; with the next chestbone 'clap' do two beats, and then do another single hand clap. It's simpler than it sounds! Try it like this:

Single chestbone clap
Single handclap
Double chestbone clap
Single hand clap

And this rhythm pattern is done **very** slowly, over and over. With even half the class doing it, it sounds great. What's more, it works very well indeed with rap poems. Jack Ousbey's 'Gran, Can You Rap?' works a treat with this – especially if you start half-way through, and break it up occasionally.

Space – When doing poems, children so often huddle together on the stage or in the performance space. Do they do this in a play? Exactly! In rehearsal, time would be well spent choreographing and noting down who can go where, who will be moving to where. (I've seen a very lively, slick version of Alan Ahlberg's 'Heard It in the Playground' by a KS2 ensemble, which was as complex as a dance, with children constantly moving across the stage as if it were a playground. Yet, this wouldn't work for all poems – many need to be static.) It might even work if some performers move into and amongst the audience.

Rehearse, rehearse, rehearse

You can do this in the classroom with the tables/chairs pushed back and, getting closer to the time/day of performance, in your school hall. It is essential that you practise beforehand in the spot on the stage where you will be performing. And really use the space. Ensure that children with the lead parts come to the front. Organise the children, and make notes of where they are standing, even moving to, if they are moving around the performance area.

By performance day, the children should know their lines off by heart. To help them to memorise them, have the words of the poem as the screensaver on the interactive board (and plaster copies all over the walls) and chant/speak them through a few times a day. Give the class copies of the poem(s) to take home. Put an enlarged copy of the poem on the classroom wall or door. Put copies up in the loo. And, as a rule of thumb, you can never rehearse too much. If the class really like the poem, children will enjoy the process.

Bring the audience into the poem

A performance should always consider its audience – the people that it is intending to entertain. With children, this may entail looking out at the audience at times, ensuring their voices are loud and clear enough to project to the area where the audience are seated. It can also mean getting the audience to join in on specific parts, say a chorus, or even do actions or gestures along with a poem. If this is the case, the audience will need to be warned beforehand and even be given a practice before the start of the piece.

A poetry performance checklist

Find a poem – What do you like about it? What does it have to say? Does it work well out loud? Why do you want others to hear it?

What is the poem about? Does it tell a story? Does it have a theme or message? How would you explain it to someone else?

How can you bring it to life? Think about these key areas:

Roles – Organise roles into… solo pairs groups ensemble

Volume – Find places to be… loud medium soft whisper

Pace – Find places to be… fast medium slow pause

Mood – Is the poem… serious funny thoughtful atmospheric

Express – Through… actions expressions gestures
props costumes music

Space – Organise performer(s) on the stage/do choreography

Rehearse, rehearse, rehrease

Bring the audience into the poem – audience participation?

Think how best to introduce the poem

Don't just say the words, mean the words

Learn the poem off by heart

Practise until it's ready

Be loud, be proud,

be ever so slightly slow and go…

for it!

Think how best to introduce the poem

An introduction does not need to be anything too elaborate, and the child/ children introducing may simply wish to inform the audience the name of the poem and the poet and who it is to be performed by. If there is time, children may wish to give some background to the piece, what it is about, why it has been chosen, and, if relevant, any audience participation that there might be.

If children are reading their own poems, they may wish to talk about the subject matter and discuss how the poem came about. It could well be that a Key Stage has decided upon a theme for the show, and may wish to open the whole performance by giving a background to the theme. Teachers themselves might choose to say a few words about what their classes have been doing in preparation.

In addition to poems, there may be drama sketches, short stories, storytelling, dance as well as live music. Poetry works well on its own or even as part of a variety show or multi-media or cross-curricular or themed event.

Don't just say the words, mean the words

This is much easier said than done. You know when a child is not doing this, because they will more than likely be reproducing the poem in a monotonic voice, one that may well doggedly accentuate the rhythm. A slow pace will help, as well as adhering to all the issues discussed above, such as pauses, changing the tone or timbre of the voice, using eye contact and gestures.

Learn the poem off by heart

As stress-inducing as this may sound to some, I'm afraid it's essential. If I can personally overcome a childhood hatred of poetry rote learning as well as a childhood stammer, and now work as a performing poet, anyone can do it! And it makes a huge difference. Once off the page, the words can come to life and take to the air, and the performer can feel that they own those words and can deliver them however they wish. Clutching a piece of paper will only be a hindrance and a distraction. Teachers or other classmates need to be on hand to give a prompt if necessary. I've seen thousands of children performing, and of the very few that falter, most of them, with encouragement, reach the end of the poem. Audiences are always warmly supportive of any child doing a poem by heart.

Practise until it's ready

As I said before, you can never practise enough and it's always good to start in the classroom, with a simple read through. From there, you can get more adventurous, assign parts and roles, push the chairs/tables back, and have read-throughs. Then a day or so before the show/assembly/performance go into the hall (or wherever the performance space may be) and get the feel of the room, use the space and project to where the audience will be. Teachers/ TAs need to stand in the audience space from time to time during a rehearsal to see if the voices are projecting into the audience space. 'A little and often' are the key words when practising. The more frequently you ask the class to run through, the tighter and slicker it will become. Good luck!

Performance suggestions for specific poems

Here are some performance suggestions for five of the poems that feature in this book. These ideas are not fixed, and merely serve as possible starting points. You may choose to use some of these ideas and then embellish with your own.

Splish! Splash! Splosh! p41

Suitable for F2, Year 1 or Year 2, this is very much a poem that comes to life in performance. As with all such poems, there are many ways it can be done. One way would be to have each verse spoken by a small group. The chorus – the Splish! Splash! Splosh! – could be done either by the whole class – whispered for the first four times it appears, then done with gusto for the last. Or, individual children could do verses, and the class could be split into 'Splish!', 'Splash!' and 'Splosh!' groups, and each group has its own action to go with their sound. In an assembly or poetry concert, these groups could wear headbands with their sounds written on them. Or thirdly, for each verse, one child could do the first line, another do the second line, another the third line, and then everyone comes in for the 'Splish! Splash! Splosh!', with this chorus going from soft on 'Splish!' to medium on 'Splash!' and to loud for 'Splosh!'. Up to the final verse, each individual line of the poem has its own image – perfect for an action or gesture. If done by the whole class, this can get messy, so perhaps those children that are not speaking certain lines could do accompanying actions. The best way is to experiment and see what works best for your class.

Happy Poem p37

Another poem for Infants. The most simple way would be for everyone to perform at the same time. But a more adventurous method might be to break the class up into groups, give them a verse each and let them work on their own actions to accompany each line. Within their groups, if there were four children, a child could do a line each. The very last two lines of the poem do lend themselves to being done by the whole class: 'happy as me' with each child pointing at themselves and 'when I'm with you' with them all pointing out at the audience.

Playgrounds p50

A poem for Lower or even Upper KS2. This poem, to give the sense of the location, needs space and, because it potentially ends on a negative note, needs a way of keeping it upbeat. If teachers are looking for solo poems, there is no reason why an individual child could not do this entire piece, but it could also be acted out by a group of children to visualise the things that are referred to in each verse – for example, in the first verse, the giggling, the whispering and the screaming and so on. To make the last line upbeat, the group that are doing the actions could come over to the child narrator and mime compassionate gestures to them. Or alternatively, each verse could be done by a different child, and at the end of the very last verse, each of the four performers could say 'Know what I mean?' together, and then hold hands. The poem would also work well if different groups perform each stanza. Probably the best bet would be to take the class into a performance space and experiment with any combination of the above suggestions from both teacher/class.

The Corn Scratch Kwa Kwa Hen and the Fox p46

A delightful free verse story poem, this could become many things in performance, including a piece led by the teacher, with the class coming in for the various animal sounds throughout, or even a piece performed by a class, with a series of different narrators. It would indeed work well done by a KS2 class as a performance for KS1/Foundation. With time, a simple set could be devised, with headbands worn by certain children, representing the different animals.

Tree p107

Before a class tackles this piece, it would be wise to type it out into verses so it can be read more easily. A perfect poem to do during the perennial 'Rainforests' topic at KS2, it could work as a solo piece, but it would also be fun to break it up and have a series of individual performers, each taking various lines. Symmetrically speaking, it would work well if one child could open and conclude the poem, perhaps even speaking a few lines within the piece too. Different children could take on other parts of the piece, and the list of wood-based artefacts that follows the line 'A tree can give an awful lot' would lend itself to a sequence of voices. So – one child could say 'the wood to make a baby's cot', another says 'pencils', the next says 'paper' and so on. Simple actions would work well too, on such lines as 'catching kites', 'dropping leaves' and so on, throughout. Whatever the pace, which would ideally be slow and steady, the ending will need to go gradually much slower, bringing it to a halt, to bring out the full effect of the last few lines.

Staging a poetry concert

Poetry concerts work on many levels: boosting confidences, encouraging creativity, developing performance, speaking and listening skills, and also **giving a chance to those children that love reading poetry out loud, but are not the best writers in the class**. It gives the latter a chance to shine, and through performing it may well have a positive impact on their writing.

Such events can also bring the whole school together, with each class performing a poem or two – as an ensemble or in groups or as individuals. Parents can be invited to watch, or even the local press could be invited to cover the event. It can be recorded for a podcast. Poems chosen for concerts can have a range of themes, or one set theme for the whole school.

Poetry anthologies group together poems of popular topics – and these could be good starting points. Here are just a few topics for finding a theme for a poetry concert: sports, school, the playground, fantasy, fairy tales, space, friends, dinosaurs, dragons, animals, minibeasts, countries of the world, travel/journeys, the seasons. Each class participating may choose to have poems from their half-term topic, thus giving the audience a taster of what each class has been learning about. Where possible, it is good to also feature poems written by the children themselves as performing to an audience is as valuable as publication, plus they receive instant feedback and gratification in a way that publication can't provide.

There could also be other elements included – children performing music and doing drama sketches or short monologues. Poetry sits so well alongside other media. Why not have your own 'Britain's Got Talent'-style show?

A poetry concert could be an annual or termly event, perhaps to coincide with National Poetry Day (first Thursday in October) or World Book Day (first Thursday in March), or whenever your book week or literacy focus events may be.

One school in Caversham had a ('Pop Idol'-inspired) KS2 Poetry Idol competition. Children themselves chose the poems, organised themselves into acts and worked up their performances. The judges? Year 5 and 6 boys (chosen by the teachers!) that rarely shone in literacy. I'm sure they won't mind you borrowing their idea.

One factor to take into consideration is the length of the event and the attention spans of the Key Stages. So, one alternative would be to have one poem from each class/year group; another alternative would be that EY and KS1 come into the hall, just for their part and then leave, or KS2 could put on a separate event.

A week or so before the event, it would be a good idea for teachers to draw up a running order of classes/poems (with appropriate timings) noting which children will introduce poems, which classes require costumes/props/music and so on.

An anthology of poems to read, discuss and perform

The anthology of poems that follows is intended to provide teachers with a

selection of poems in a variety of forms, styles and voices, to generate discussion and creative responses. Some poems are ideal for performances. I have not signalled which are good for quiet reading or discussion or performing, or even which ages they might be suitable for. That is for teachers and their classes to decide.

It goes without saying that it is vital that children read and hear a lot of poetry. We can't expect children to love poetry, to write their own poetry, to perform poetry, if they have not had a healthy and regular diet of verse. To this end, at the back of the book, I have created a short list of some poems/poets that work well in Primary schools. Please feel free to find what you think is suitable for your class. As I always say, time spent with verse will also reap many benefits with children's prose reading and writing.

There are three poems by contemporary writers:

- Julie Holder's 'The Corn Scratch Kwa Kwa Hen and the Fox' is a charming, longer free verse narrative piece. It would suit F/KS1, with a teacher as narrator with children joining in with animal actions and sounds; or for Lower KS2, a group of children as narrators, with the rest of the class providing sound effects and actions, or even acting out the scenario.

- Berlie Doherty's 'Playgrounds' explores a topic that all school children can easily identify with. It is perfect for an ensemble performance, with different voices/groups doing a verse each.

- Brian Moses' 'Heaven' could generate some wonderful, thoughtful and philosophical discussions and would lend itself well to a solo or small group performance.

'The Listeners' by Walter de la Mare is chosen because it is a classic poem that will hopefully encourage teachers to consider poems by poets such as Eleanor Farjeon, James Reeves, Robert Louis Stevenson, Lewis Carroll, A. A. Milne, Alfred Noyes, Charles Causely, and many others.

As you read through these poems, you could consider:

- Which poem could compliment a current topic/curricular area?

- Which poem would be of interest to my class?

- Which poem would give them something to perform, in class or an assembly or a concert?

- Which poem might serve as a good writing model?

- Which poem could be poem of the day/week/month?

- Which poem could I copy and put up in the staffroom/corridor/interactive white board and/or as a screensaver or on the school intranet?

- Which poem would be good for sharing, reading aloud and discussing?

Overall, I encourage teachers to use some of these but to look widely for poems (see LET'S LIVE POETRY: The poetry classroom p14), as there are many great poems out there written for children – classic, contemporary, in a whole range of tones, moods, forms, styles and voices. Enjoy!

Happy Poem

Happy as a rainbow
happy as a bee
happy as a dolphin
splashing in the sea

Happy as bare feet
running on the beach
happy as a sunflower
happy as a peach

Happy as a poppy
happy as a spoon
dripping with honey
happy as June

Happy as a banjo
plucking on a tune
happy as a Sunday
lazy afternoon

Happy as a memory
shared by two
happy as me . . .
when I'm with you!

James Carter
(Hey, Little Bug! Frances Lincoln)

rhyming poem

Zim Zam Zoom!

Brown rocket
green rocket
first I've seen rocket
best there's ever been rocket

ZIM ZAM ZOOM!

Rush rocket
roar rocket
zip about some more rocket
let me climb aboard rocket

ZIM ZAM ZOOM!

Blast rocket
fast rocket
overtaking Mars rocket
heading for the stars rocket

ZIM ZAM ZOOM!

Red rocket
blue rocket
racing to the moon rocket
won't you come back soon rocket

ZIM ZAM ZOOM!

James Carter

rhyming poem with a chorus

Saturn!

I love the stars
the MOON the SUN
but Saturn you're
my number 1

Your rings are pearls
from deep blue seas
baubles hung
from Christmas trees
CANDLES in a
hoop of heaven
crystals in a
gloomy cavern

With your fancy
silver rings
Saturn you're
The King
of
BLING!

James Carter
(with Madeleine Carter)

rhyming poem with calligrams

Pirate Pete

Pirate Pete
had a ship on the sea
had a fish for his tea
had a peg for a knee
        and a tiny little parrot called . . . Polly

Pirate Pete
had a book with a map
had a skull on his cap
had a cat on his lap
        and another little parrot called . . . Dolly

Pirate Pete
had a trunk full of treasure
had a belt made of leather
had a cap with a feather
        and another little parrot called . . . Jolly

Pirate Pete
had a patch on his eye
had a flag he would fly
had a plank way up high
        and another little parrot called . . . Molly

So Pirate Pete
  and the parrots four
   they sailed the world
    from shore to shore –
    collecting gold
     and gifts galore.
      And that's their tale –
     there is no more!

James Carter
(Hey, Little Bug! Frances Lincoln)

rhyming poem

Splish! Splash! Splosh!

Babies in the bath do it
puddles on the path do it
grannies for a laugh do it

SPLISH! SPLASH! SPLOSH!

Dirty welly boots do it
dainty little shoes do it
drippy doggies too do it

SPLISH! SPLASH! SPLOSH!

Waterfalls and waves do it
giant killer whales do it
little fishes' tails do it

SPLISH! SPLASH! SPLOSH!

Buses rushing past do it
rivers flowing fast do it
raindrops fall at last do it

SPLISH! SPLASH! SPLOSH!

Swimmers in the pool do it
penguins in the zoo do it
dolphins in the blue do it

SPLISH! SPLASH! SPLOSH!

In the summer sun do it
do it as it's fun do it
come on everyone do it

SPLISH!
SPLASH!
SPLOSH!

James Carter
(Hey, Little Bug! Frances Lincoln)

rhyming poem with a chorus

Wild, Wild Weather

On a wild, wild walk
a while ago

We climbed a hill
we turned a bend
we crossed a stream
we stopped and then . . . SNOW!

Big snow thick snow
snow you could lick snow
white snow bright snow
snow snow snow!

CHORUS: We climbed . . . WIND!

Big wind warm wind
blowing up a storm wind
high wind wild wind
wind wind wind!

CHORUS: We climbed . . . RAIN!

Big rain wet rain
hard as you can get rain
warm rain storm rain
rain rain rain!

CHORUS: We climbed . . . MIST!

Big mist white mist
oh what a sight mist
high mist wide mist
mist mist mist!

CHORUS: We climbed . . . SUN!

Big sun hot sun
oh what a lot sun
bright sun light sun
sun sun sun!

It all began with a fall of snow –
on a wild, wild walk
a while ago

James Carter

rhyming poem with a chorus

Where Did We Go?

We bought a ticket to... Kalamazoo
we went by train
by boat, by plane
around the world
and back again
through night and day
through sun and rain
through mist and snow... Then where did we go?

We bought a ticket to... Timbuktu
we went by train
by boat by plane... Then where did we go?

We bought a ticket to... Kathmandu
we went by train
by boat by plane... Then where did we go?

We bought a ticket to [you choose some places]
we went by train
by boat by plane...

Then where did we go?

[Last verse]

We bought a ticket to Kalamazoo
    to Timbuktu
    to Kathmandu
    to [your places]

we went by train
by boat, by plane
around the world
and back again
through night and day
through sun and rain
through mist and snow

Then where did we go?

Home
    sweet
        home ! ! !

James Carter
(Hey, Little Bug! Frances Lincoln)

rhyming poem with a chorus

43

What Am I?
(a kingsize kenning)

sea-lover
>beach-hater

deep-diver
>wave-maker

great-gusher
>super-crusher

tail-flipper
>big-dipper

boat-tipper
>sea-sipper

To make a splash
>I never fail
Have you guessed?
>I'm a...whale!

James Carter

kenning

We Are Learning To...

& What I'm Looking For

On our first day
in our new class
our new teacher
wrote two words
on the board:

WALT and WILF

and then she asked us,
'Does anyone know
what these
stand for?'

We were all
very quiet.

Then all of a sudden
my hand shot up
and I shrieked,

'Miss! MISS! is it...
What A Lovely Teacher
and
We Is Learning Fings?'

And everyone laughed,
e s p e c i a l l y our teacher!

James Carter

free verse poem

The Corn Scratch Kwa Kwa Hen and the Fox

And the Corn Scratch Kwa Kwa Hen
heard the grumbling rumbling belly
of the Slink Back Brush Tail Fox
a whole field away.

And she said to her sisters in the henhouse,
'Sisters, that Slink Back Brush Tail Fox
will come and here's what to do,'
and she whispered in their sharp sharp ears, 'kwa, kwa.'

And when that Slink Back Brush Tail Fox
came over the fields at night,
she heard his paw slide on a leaf,
and the Corn Scratch Kwa Kwa Hen and her sisters
opened their beaks and –

'KWA!'
The moon jumped
and the Chooky Chook Chicks
hid under the straw and giggled,
It was the LOUDEST KWA in the world.

And the Log Dog and the Scat Cat
and the Brat Rat and the House Mouse
and the Don't Harm Her Farmer
and his Life Wife and their Shorter Daughter
and their One Son came running.
On their slip slop, flip flop,
scatter clatter, slick flick, tickly feet
and they opened their mouths and shouted –

'FOX!'
And it was the loudest name in the world.
And the Slink Back Brush Tail Fox
ran over the fields and far away
and hid in a hole with his grumbling rumbling belly.

And the Corn Scratch Kwa Kwa Hen
tucked the Chooky Chook Chicks under her feathers
and said 'kwa,'
and it was the softest kwa in the world.

Julie Holder

free verse poem

Take A Poem

Why not take a poem
wherever you go?
Pop it in your pocket
nobody will know

Take it to your classroom
stick it on the wall
tell them all about it
read it in the hall

Take it to the bathroom
tuck it up in bed
take the time to learn it
keep it in your head

Take it for a day trip
take it on a train
fold it as a hat
when it starts to rain

Take it to a river
fold it as a boat
pop it in the water
hope that it will float

Take it to a hilltop
fold it as a plane
throw it up skywards
time and time again

Take it to a postbox
send it anywhere
out into the world
with
     tender
        loving
           care

James Carter
(Time-travelling Underpants,
Macmillan Children's Books)

rhyming poem

I Asked The Little Boy Who Can't See

I asked the little boy who can't see,
'And what is colour like?'
'Why, green,' said he,
'Is like the rustle when the wind blows through
the forest; running water, that is blue;
and red is like a trumpet sound; and pink
is like the smell of roses; I think
that purple must be like a thunderstorm;
and yellow is like something soft and warm;
and white is a pleasant stillness when you lie
and dream.'

Anon

rhyming poem

If, If, If...

If the sea was in the sky,
and trees were underground,
and if all fish had giant teeth,
and all the cows were round,
if birds flew backwards all the time,
and vultures ruled the land,
if bricks poured down instead of rain,
if all there was was sand,
if every man had seven heads,
and we spoke Double Dutch,
and if the sun came out at night,
I wouldn't like it much.

Anon

rhyming poem

Playgrounds

Playgrounds are such gobby places.
Know what I mean?
Everyone seems to have something to
Talk about, giggle, whisper, scream and shout about,
I mean, it's like being in a parrot cage.

And playgrounds are such pushy places.
Know what I mean?
Everyone seems to have to
Run about, jump, kick, do cartwheels, handstands, fly around,
I mean, it's like being inside a whirlwind.

And playgrounds are such patchy places.
Know what I mean?
Everyone seems to
Go round in circles, lines and triangles, coloured shapes,
I mean it's like being in a kaleidoscope.

And playgrounds are such pally places.
Know what I mean?
Everyone seems to
Have best friends, secrets, link arms, be in gangs,
Everyone, except me.

Know what I mean?

Berlie Doherty
(Walking On Air,
Hodder Children's Books)

free verse poem

Night Soup

Take . . .

A slither of moon
a nip in the air
a sprinkle of stars
a creak from a stair

Add plenty of dark
the slink of a cat
(with cold green eyes)
a loop from a bat

The patter of rain
the whine of a dog
the taste of a dream
the wisp of a fog

The whoosh of a train
a sniff or a snore
the swoop of an owl
then stop – no more

Then stir it around
and bring to the boil
season with cinnamon
add olive oil

Now let it go cold
and serve quite late
and all
        that is left
                to do
                    is wait...

James Carter
(Time-travelling Underpants,
Macmillan Children's Books)

rhyming/list poem

This Is Where...

...I learnt to be.
And this is where I learnt to read,
and write and count and act in plays,
and blossom in so many ways...

And this is where I learnt to sing,
express myself, and really think.
And this is where I learnt to dream,
to wonder why and what things mean.

And this is where I learnt to care,
to make good friends, to give, to share,
to kick, to catch, to race, to run.
This is where I had such fun.

And this is where I grew and grew.
And this is where? My Primary school.

James Carter
(Journey to the Centre of My Brain,
Macmillan Children's Books)

rhyming poem

Heaven

From the top of Breakneck Hill
we thought we might see Heaven,
some space between clouds where light pours through,
the place where the chosen ones would go.

We didn't know, of course, what Heaven looked like:
there were no tourist guides
and no-one who went there
came back to tell.

Most of us hoped it would be an endless funfair,
a sweetstore where you'd help yourself
again and again,
a Saturday treat or the sort of holiday
that would last forever.

Even the clever ones at school
had no more idea of what Heaven might be,
although Sam, who lived for numbers,
said that in all probability it would be
an endless maths lesson.

We pitied him, and thought that such a geeky response
didn't warrant any reply.

So we watched the clouds play tag
across an arc of sky,
then set off home.

Heaven could wait…
there was Doctor Who on TV soon,
wouldn't that be Heaven enough
for one afternoon?

Brian Moses
(Holding the Hands of
Angels, Salt Publishing)

free verse poem

53

The Ancient Greeks...

knew a thing
  or two
    about m o n s t e r s.

From their minds
        their mouths
            their myths
came c r e a t u r e s
        that still haunt us
            taunt us
                today.

Beware of the dog:
            the three-headed C e r b e r u s
                that guards the gates
                    of the underworld.

Keep your eyes on the bull:
                with the body of a man
                    he's as strong as he is tall
                        the menacing M i n o t a u r.

It's rude to stare
        at M e d u s a
            with her snakes-for-hair
            one look alone
                will turn you to cold stone.

There are more besides
            and what's for sure
                they don't make b e a s t s
                    like these anymore.

James Carter

free verse poem with some rhymes

dinosaurs were real, then maybe
dragons were as well. And perhaps
one day soon they'll find a skeleton
beside a cliff, inside a cave:
a backbone, a tail, a massive head,
and those branch-like bones
where the wings would have been;
or even a whole beast, perfectly
preserved in Siberian snow:
grey-green and scaly, those two top
canine fangs just jutting over the jaw,
the raging fire of the beast long lost
to the deep sleep of the dead,
those saggy eyelids closed
forever.

James Carter
(Journey to the Centre of My Brain,
Macmillan Children's Books)

free verse poem

Talking Teeth

My dentist, Pete, has a real
mammoth tooth fossil. He keeps it
in his cupboard. It cost him ten quid.
It's a molar, and an ugly, rusty, lump
of a thing, as big and as chunky
as a brick. The tooth's got
these deep ridges, just right
for grinding leaves and grasses.
It's one hundred thousand
years old, yet it doesn't have
a single filling.

Wish I was a woolly mammoth!

James Carter

free verse poem

Words

Go tell the world
    that words aren't cheap

for like the trees
    their roots go deep

for like the winds
    they blow your way

for like the seeds
    they won't all stay

for like the clouds
    they have such grace

for like the seas
    they roar and rage

for like the sun
    they feed you light

for like the moon
    they dwell at night

for like the sky
    they're made of air

go tell the world
    treat words with care

James Carter
(Time-travelling Underpants,
Macmillan Children's Books)

rhyming poem

Love You More

Do I love you
to the moon and back?
No I love you
more than that

I love you to the desert sands
the mountains, stars
the planets and

I love you to the deepest sea
and deeper still
through history

Before beyond I love you then
I love you now
I'll love you when

The sun's gone out
the moon's gone home
and all the stars are fully grown

When I no longer say these words
I'll give them to the wind, the birds
so that they will still be heard

I love you

James Carter
(Time-travelling Underpants,
Macmillan Children's Books)

rhyming poem

Night Cat (for Jacob)

Where are you heading tonight, Cat?
Wandering over the garden walls?
With click of the claws and pad of the paws,
and swish of the tail and snap of the jaws?

Magical. That's what you are.
With eyes like orbs of seagreen glass.
With whiskers white to match the stars.

Where are you heading tonight, Cat?
You're swift as fox and wise as owl,
you're slick, you are, you slink, you prowl.
Oh, you own the night, and how.

You're über-animal. Simple as that.
You're top-of-the-heap in your habitat.
You're mystical too, you mag-nif-i-cat!

Where are you heading tonight, Cat?
Down the alleyways, out of sight?
Into the heart and soul of night?
Where dark's so dark it turns to light?

And with your rowdy, meowly tune,
will you charm your mistress moon?
I miss you, kitty. Come home soon.
Where are you heading tonight, Cat?

James Carter

rhyming poem with a chorus

The Story of Water

Once, the earth, like the moon,
  was a desert-dry and stony place.

This so saddened the sky that she cried seven tears
  to fall to earth
   to make the waters of the world.

  The first tear formed the glistening streams.
The second tear formed the mighty rivers.
  The third tear formed the glassy lakes.
The fourth tear formed the salty seas.
  The fifth tear formed the endless oceans.
The sixth tear formed the giant ice caps.
  The seventh tear turned to clouds
            to create more water
             whenever it was needed.

The sky saw
 the waters were still
  so she moaned and she groaned
   and she wailed and she howled
    thus forming the very first winds.

The sky was pleased
 for she saw that the waters
  would always be wrapped in waves.

So the wind
 and the clouds
  and the waters and the waves were born
   leaving time to start working
    on life . . .

James Carter

narrative free verse poem

Porky Pies! or The Three Little Pigs Rap

CHORUS: 'I'll huff, I'll puff I'll blow you down
I'll blow you guys right out of town!'
No Wolfie said that dreadful stuff
or treated little piglets rough!

I'll tell you something just for free
about them little piglets 3
I'll spill the beans on porky pies
those saucy piglets' naughty lies

Huffing? Puffing? Come on, please!
Poor Wolfie had a dreadful sneeze.
Well, hay fever to be precise –
his nose was red – as were his eyes. CHORUS

When Wolfie sniffed that house of hay
he sneezed the little place away
then same again at pighouse 2 –
his nostrils twitched and twitched... ATCHOO!!!
CHORUS

That house of straw was now no more
a pile of stuff upon the floor –
then Wolfie strolled around da hood
and found a place that looked real good. CHORUS

And built of bricks and built to last
he hurried up the garden path
to get a tissue for his snout
he knocked and knocked – but were they out?
CHORUS

Did Wolfie trash that pighouse 3?
or end up Wolfie R.I.P.?
or boiled alive by piglets 3?
well – NO, NO, NO – the truth you see. CHORUS

Poor Wolfie left to find out if
some quack could cure his Summer sniff
and after that was seen no more
by pigs with bricks and hay and straw. CHORUS

I'm out of puff – but here's the deal
dem fibs ain't cool – KEEP IT REAL!

James Carter

rap

The Listeners

'Is there anybody there?' said the Traveller,
Knocking on the moonlit door;
And his horse in the silence champ'd the grasses
Of the forest's ferny floor:
And a bird flew up out of the turret,
Above the Traveller's head:
And he smote upon the door again a second time;
'Is there anybody there?' he said.
But no one descended the Traveller;
No head from the leaf-fringed sill
Lean'd over and look'd into his grey eyes,
Where he stood perplex'd and still.
But only a host of phantom listeners
That dwelt in the lone house then
Stood listening in the quiet of the moonlight
To that voice from the world of men:
Stood thronging the faint moonbeams on the dark stair,
That goes down to the empty hall,
Hearkening in an air stirr'd and shaken
By the lonely Traveller's call.
And he felt in his heart their strangeness,
Their stillness answering his cry,
While his horse moved, cropping the dark turf,
'Neath the starr'd and leafy sky;
For he suddenly smote on the door, even
Louder, and lifted his head:–
'Tell them I came, and no one answer'd,
That I kept my word,' he said.
Never the least stir made the listeners,
Though every word he spake
Fell echoing through the shadowiness of the still house
From the one man left awake:
Ay, they heard his foot upon the stirrup,
And the sound of iron on stone,
And how the silence surged softly backward,
When the plunging hoofs were gone.

Walter de la Mare

rhyming poem

Section Three - Writing poetry

Let's Play

Poetry warm-ups and games

or as starting points before going on to work through the LET'S WRITE POETRY workshops that follow.

Foundation and Infant classes learn so much through constructive play, and it is through play and a playful approach to their art that professional writers create, craft and develop their work. They consider 'What if... '; they play the game of 'Let's pretend'. In the same way, writing at both KS1 and KS2 needs to retain some of the playfulness that is intrinsic to the Early Years as that, essentially, is where ideas grow from. Poets in particular look to see what happens when they play with language, put words together and see how they sound, they flow, they sing, and what new meanings are created when different words/ phrases are used. As many educationalists have already pointed out, young children are innate poets, instinctively enjoying the textures and rhythms of language, seeing the world afresh with wonder. It's that point of view, that mindset, that poets need to find themselves in and hence the need for this section!

The ideas that follow can be used for all kinds of purposes and contexts – **but they all have the express intention of getting classes in a playful and creative frame of mind for writing**. Some are intended as quick games, others could easily be extended into full poems. Many of these can be done as activities in their own right,

Alliterating alphabet/ tongue-twisters

Either as a one-off activity or as a one-a-day journey through the alphabet, pick a letter and write the longest phrase you can, using only words that begin with that letter e.g. Frank's friend Fred found four fat frogs feeding furiously/Curiously, Carl's cousin couldn't catch cod. As you can see, these make fun tongue-twisters too!

Alliterating story

AS I zoomed around the zoo
I saw one w....
Two t....
Three th...

AS I shuffled around the shops
I saw one w...

AS I swam beneath the sea
I saw one w...
Two t

Feel free to add extra alliterative adjectives, verbs and adverbs.

Animal warning rhymes

These are so simple. Rather than end-rhymes, these lines use rhymes-within-the-lines. Try some! Maybe brainstorm some bugs and animals and look for rhymes:

> Take CARE near a BEAR.
> Don't have TEA with a BEE.
> Don't grab the TALE of a WHALE.

Assonant animals

Assonance is similar to alliteration, but is about the sound inside each word:

The CROSS WASP stung the BLACK CAT.

The YOUNG SLUG slimes down the DARK PATH.

The SAD CRAB HAD no SNACK.

Say these words out loud – CROSS/WASP and BLACK/CAT and you will hear the same internal sound, the assonance. Now think of some of your own.

The book of dreams

Musician/comedian Bill Bailey does a fantastic sketch about the Argos catalogue, in which he calls it 'The Book of Dreams'. So, borrowing Bill's great idea, imagine what would be in such a book...

In the Book of Dreams

I found...
a unicorn cantering into a wood
an ocean awash with starlight
a dragon nesting a crimson egg...

Calligrams

A calligram is a word that is made to look like what it is, for example:

BIG

small

W I D E

CURVY

Read the calligram poem 'Saturn' on p39.

Have fun drawing or writing calligram phrases:

The TALL QUEEN

The w l   w n   b e
        i d   i d   l w

A further calligram workshop is on p106.

Daisychain - five word story

A very popular, very simple idea: you write a five word story, beginning with 'The'. From there, the last letter of that word becomes the first letter of the next word: 'The e...'. They don't have to make sense necessarily. 'The elegant teacher rarely yodels.' or 'The endless sand drifted downwards.'

Dreamers' dreams

Kenneth Koch's book 'Rose, Where Did You Get That Red?' is full of marvels, including the origins of this exercise. It's very simple, and can be as elaborate as you wish. Each child could do a few lines, and contribute to one massive class poem!

When day is done
and night has come
that's when dreamers dream...

A tree dreams
of a winter coat
A caterpillar dreams
of a life with wings

Food poems

I meet innovative teachers that look around for poems that can act as good models for children's own writing. This is what happened at St John the Evangelist CE Infant School in Newbury. Using my own poem 'Splish! Splash! Splosh!' p41, the children were asked to write their own version using 'Munch Crunch Munch!' as the chorus. Note how every line uses an expressive verb – 'munching', 'chomping' etc. – rather than 'eating'. Great poem, Laura!

Rabbits munching on carrots do it
owls slurping on worms do it
dogs gnawing on bones do it

Munch Crunch Munch!

Horses chomping on apples do it
giraffes nibbling on leaves do it
penguins dining on fish do it

Munch Crunch Munch!

extract by Laura, Year 2 class, St John the Evangelist CE Infant School, Newbury

Gifts for a nowhere world

Many schools send out shoeboxes with gifts inside at Christmas time. This poem is akin to such a Christmas box. Inspired by a favourite Beatles' song (John Lennon's sublime 'Nowhere Man') it encourages children to creatively employ the five senses. Below, there are the gifts of touch and sound, and a number of these use alliteration to give extra texture to the line.

To a nowhere world
I would send . . .

the crunch of a cornflake
the sizzle of a sausage
the clink and the clank of car keys

the bristle of a caterpillar
the tickle of a cat's tongue
the warm kiss of a midday sun

I used to...

Kenneth Koch time again. This one is great for children comparing themselves to how they used to be. It's a simple structure: 'I used to... but now I... '. Perhaps, 'I used to swim with a rubber ring but now I can swim sixteen lengths.' As with 'rubber ring' and 'swim sixteen', try and use some alliteration. You could adapt this to 'I used to like/love... but now I like/love... '.

Mini animal simile poems

Pick an animal. Brainstorm all of its features. Now be adventurous. What are those features like? For example, Shark: teeth/skin/fin/tail/jaws:

Shark

Teeth as jagged as broken glass
Skin as smooth as a clear blue pool
Fin as sharp as a midnight mountain... and so on

Pangrams

These can be tricky, but they're great fun. Pangrams are short phrases that use all or as many of the 26 letters of the alphabet as possible, such as in the typesetter's phrase:

The quick brown fox jumps over the lazy dog.

To use up the more obscure letters, like 'q', 'x' and 'z', try coming up with names like Max Quigly or Zak McQueen. Or even try writing a pangram with only invented words. If your first version contains many sentences, in a second version try and cut this down as much as you can.

Six ways into the ocean

This model uses a number of poetic forms to explore a topic, and borrows from Wallace Stevens' fabulous poem 'Thirteen Ways of Looking at a Blackbird'. In the following example the topic of water is explored as: One is a simple rhyme, two is an acrostic, three is a rhyming haiku, four is a kenning, five is a rhyming riddle, and six is a shape poem.

This multi-form approach could be used with all kinds of popular topics, such as Rainforests, Minibeasts, Animals, Pirates – and would make a great display.

ONE

It's deep it's damp it's big it's blue
it's green it's grey it's turquoise too
It's freezing cold and wild and yet
It could be called the world wide wet!

TWO

octOpus
Crab
jEllyfish
shArk
dolphiN

THREE

Here, there, gone again
    ever moving through a chain
stream - river - sea - rain

FOUR

beach-licker
   Ship-Sinker
      deep-thinker
         cliff-breaker
           life-taker
             cloud-maker

FIVE

My first's in COD
but not in PLAICE
My second's in CRAB
though not in HAKE
My third you'll find
is there in the SEA -
(as well as my fourth)
But finally,
my fifth's in TITANIC...
So tragic!

SIX

```
        r
      i
    v
  e
r
  r
    i
      v
        e
          r
            o
           oc
           oce
           ocea
           ocean
           oceanocean
         oceanoceanocean
       oceanoceanoceanoceanocean
```

Snapshot of the seasons: metaphors

Each season has to be represented by a simple, single image. Try using different senses. Even do four or so lines per season:

Spring is a shoot of green
Summer is a kiss of sun
Autumn is a leaf of bronze
Winter is a field of snow

Similes

The best similes sound fresh and take risks. Children can find these hard initially, but given time, they can come out with some amazing similes. Try this fun exercise and see what your class comes up with:

Have You Seen My Dragon?

He's as
ANGRY as ...
FIERY as ...
TALL as ...
WIDE as ...
FLABBY as ...
QUICK as ...
CRUEL as ...
BRAVE as ...
WILD as ...
EVIL as a ...
LOVEABLE as ...

with claws as ... as ...
with jaws as ... as ...
with a tail as ... as ...
with wings as ... as ...
with breath as ... as ...

Feel free to add extra adjectives, and pick a pet/beast/monster/alien/Gruffalo of your own.

Super similes

This is a very simple exercise to encourage children to think and write in a fresh way. Ask them to write two or three words per line. Often a first thought or idea will be a cliché, but the second or third will hopefully be more original and adventurous. Feel free to add/delete adjectives.

Hey, look at me

I'm...
Cool as a ...
Cute as a ...
Hot as a ...
Bouncy as a ...
Sticky as a ...
Flat as a ...
Tall as a ...
Short as a ...
Stripy as a ...
Spotty as a ...
Speedy as a ...
That's me!

Tell me lies

This workshop of old uses questions and answers to make a great structure for a poem. Ask the class to think of some questions about the world and the universe. For example: What is the sea? Why is the moon grey? Where do clouds go at night? The answers have to be imaginative and not scientific. Here are some more: Where does space end? When did time begin? Where does the wind come from?

Utter nonsense

Read the poem 'If, If, If...' on p49. Write your own rhyming or non-rhyming version. Try brainstorming some ideas first. Look out the window. What is the world like? What is the opposite of our world like? If there was another Earth out there in the universe, in what ways would it be different?

Rhyme practices

Children love rhyming, but it's not easy to write good rhymes. Regular practice is essential! And it's always useful to do a quick practice rhyme as a warm-up before children then go on to write their own rhyming poems.

See LET'S WRITE POETRY FOR A REASON: Rhyme practices, p78.

Utterly magical animals - even more nonsense

This is a workshop I borrowed and adapted from Brian Moses, who in turn took his inspiration from Kenneth Patchen's fabulously surreal poem, 'The Magical Mouse'. First of all we created a brainstorm of what cats do – eat, walk, prowl, purr, eat, meow etc, and then I set up the following structure on the board - 'I am the Magical Cat! I don't.../ I..., I don't / I...' . The intention is to use language creatively with alliteration aplenty!

The Magical Cat

I am the Magical Cat!
I don't eat meat or mice.
I choke as I chew
            on frogs' legs
                and dragons' wings.
I have snakes as my tail.
I don't leap,
        I don't creep,
            I don't scamper around...
I can fly with my wobbly white wings
            to Wonderland...
                where the frogs eat logs
                and dragonflies turn
                into dragons!
I don't meow or purr. No!
I squawk like an eagle.
I ting like a triangle.
And late at night
        I like to sing
        'I am the Magical Cat!'

**Lauren Carter, Yr 3,
South Moreton Primary School**

Let's Write Poetry

Teacher as scribe/ Running a poetry workshop

Poets say that you can't teach how to write poetry. However, they would all agree that you can certainly show a class all the things that poetry can be as well as demonstrate the process of how poetry can be written. The more frequently you can do this, the more children will understand the stages and creative processes involved. You can write collaboratively – as an integral part of most poetry workshops, and this is much simpler than it sounds – honestly! Teachers create text on the board with children every single day. Invariably, this will be prose. So, the leap to writing a communal poem with a class should, in theory, be minimal. All it takes is for you to spend time familiarising yourself with the particular poetic form chosen, and to practise beforehand and even read out your own poem (if you wish to) to inspire the class.

Children and teachers alike need to recognise that creativity is often a messy and random process. Look at roughs and drafts and revisions of poems. Find the versions of 'How To Build A Dragon' on p116. There is the final draft as well the first/second draft; the latter has both typed and hand-written text. Scan these onto the interactive board and ask children to compare the differences and ask why the final version is better and in what ways.

In an ideal world, by KS2 children would be given the freedom of a whole hour of freestyle, creative writing – that's a whole hour to forget about structures and formulas and spelling and punctuation and grammar. It's a whole hour to get lost in their writing, to write unconsciously, to write uninhibited and to find out the kind of writers that they can be. Ideally, by Year 5 or Year 6, children will have had experience of free verse, haikus, kennings and many other forms and would be able to choose the poetic form to suit their subject matter. A heron gliding over a river? A haiku. Henry VIII? A kenning… or a rap! An early memory at the seaside? A free verse poem. But all this comes with time and practice and regular exposure to poetry. For now, let's look at a basic structure of a poetry writing workshop.

A basic workshop structure

To begin a workshop, you will need to explain the structure and features of the chosen form/poem to be written, and then act as scribe, and work on a poem with your class in that form to show in a certain amount of detail how it is constructed. How to go about scribing/composing a communal class poem is shown implicitly in many of the workshops that follow in LET'S WRITE POETRY FOR A REASON. (I use the word 'workshop' throughout as creative writing sessions are, by their nature, workshops and not 'lessons'.)

Yet you do not have to follow the recommended stages below word for word, and might well find a methodology that works better for them. Also, it might be relevant in some cases to part-scribe a poem. If a Year 6 teacher wanted her class to write their own Victorians rap for instance, she might choose to write a communal opening – say one or two rhyming couplets and let the class work from those.

A workshop, like any 'lesson', needs to have some kind of coherent structure, and will vary depending on the teacher's style, the children/ages involved and even the form/subject of the poem. Here is one such structure that you can adopt and adapt:

Stage 1 – Inform
Stage 2 – Read
Stage 3 – Brainstorm
Stage 4 – Time to talk?
Stage 5 – Time to write
Stage 6 – Time to reflect
Stage 7 – Publish

Stage 1 - Inform

Inform the class as to what they will be writing, and to what the expectations of the workshop will be. For example, 'Today, because our topic is space, we will be writing poems about the sun. The type of poem we will write will be a haiku. By the end of the session, each of you will have started a first draft of a haiku poem.'

Stage 2 - Read

Read the class a model or two. One of these might be from a poetry book, the other by you. If the latter, you might choose to explain how the poem came about, how the poem took shape and how you reflect on the poem now. Children need to see that teachers are writers too!

Once read, you can highlight the main features of the poem. For example if it is a haiku, you could explain that the poem has three lines, and is made up of seventeen syllables, and so on.

To extend this further, you may wish to have the model poem on a permanent display in your classroom. If you are working on syllabic poetry one week, to explore your topic of nature for instance, you could put up a display of haikus, tankas and cinquains. This means that for the whole period, children will be both actively reading as well as passively absorbing information about those poems. You could even invite members of the class to read out their favourite poems from the display.

Stage 3 - Brainstorm

If you plan for the class to a) write in a specific form and b) on a specific topic, it is vital to brainstorm ideas and subject knowledge on that topic first. So, if the workshop is to focus on sun haikus, you could do a spider diagram brainstorming key words/thoughts on that topic. The key questions What? When? Where? Why? How? might bring out some useful material.

Many younger classes will find it helpful to have a title, a phrase or an opening line to start with, and you may need to prepare one or even a few of these beforehand.

If you decide that the workshop will be based on a poetic form, but for the subject to be free choice, it would again be useful to brainstorm ideas. So, if the chosen form is kennings, and you have given the class carte blanche to write about their own subject, then it would be good to write down a list of topics that the children could choose from – for example, animals, the elements, sports people, celebrities.

Stage 4 - Time to talk?

The vogue nowadays is for children to talk through their ideas before they write about them. This is valuable, and frequently achieves good results, as it helps to shape, refine, clarify and expand their ideas. Yet, when it comes to creative writing, some children can feel that having talked about it, they've lost the impetus to then go on and write about it. How many times have you met someone at a party that tells you about the book they plan to write? Do they do it? Exactly!

Stage 5 - Time to write

An insightful quote from a child, 'I don't know what I think until I've written it' reveals that writing is and should be **a process of discovery**. Children need time and space to discover and explore. It's what I call 'getting lost in the fog of creativity'. As a reader you get immersed in another world, and so it is for a writer too, and all this takes quality time. Perhaps you could stipulate that there will be uninterrupted writing for a set period of time – i.e. no fussing, looking for rubbers, no worrying about spellings.

How long this should be will depend on the age of the class/abilities/attention spans, and for the teacher to decide what is appropriate. However, it is good to have some of this time, where possible, in silence. Some teachers even choose to have gentle ambient music playing in the background. This is a great idea. It settles the class, focuses the creative mind, and nurtures innovation.

It is also crucial that children know that their writing from a workshop will not be 'marked' for formal writing skills – i.e. punctuation, spellings, neatness. As Bernard Ashley so wisely says, 'Don't get it right, get it written!' You could even put this quote on the whiteboard to focus and reassure the class that they are not striving for perfection every time they commit pen to paper.

When you are writing a story, it will ideally need a plan of some sort, just to get you started. But a poem could begin with all kinds of things, and that will depend on the workshop itself and the input from you. It might be knowing the form you will write (e.g. haiku, cinquain or rap), or the structure you will use, or a set theme or even a title and an opening line or two. Alternatively, it might be a free writing session and the choice of what to write might be up to individual children. Children do need scope to write whatever they want to on occasion.

Children will need to daydream their ideas for a while, mull over them, gaze out the window and think it all through. As far as I can see, having watched a great many children writing over the last twenty years, nothing is more productive and ultimately creative than picking up a pen and getting on with it. How do you find out what you are going to write? There's only one true way – by writing!

Some children will be working with a Learning Support Assistant. Some will need you to come and lend ideas and support. Ideally (and I say 'ideally'), you would write alongside the class. I have met many teachers that swear by this, and they feel it's good for them and the children – being able to show that he is a writer too, and can share the frustrations/joys/successes/rewards etc. of writing.

Stage 6 - Time to reflect

Time does need to be built in so that some of the children can read out their work, and be given an opportunity to reflect on what they've written, and even for other children to comment – critically and positively – on their peer's writing. By listening, enjoying and relishing each other's writing, it helps to build a supportive network of young readers/writers. This is one of the most essential stages in a workshop; it is a vital thing for children to work together as a community of writers/listeners/appreciators of each other's work. To this end, every child should receive a hearty round of applause every time they read out a new poem.

If an older class, say Years 5 and 6, they could even work in pairs as 'Response Partners', responding critically but positively on their partner's work, and you could ask them to a) 'find three things they like', and b) 'two things that could do with more work'.

Tweaking

As a teacher of Years 5 or 6, you might build in a system by which the first workshop is to explore ideas and to be creative, and in a second session the intention is to develop, expand, write more, but also 'tweak' and draft. Needless to say, children hate the word 'drafting' but never seem to complain about the word 'tweak'. You might even want to signal what areas could be 'tweaked', for example, weak adjectives such as 'nice', 'beautiful', 'spooky', 'scary', clichés and awkward phrases, as well as lumpy rhythms and lazy rhymes. (All these are covered in LET'S RESPOND TO POETRY: Poetry checklist on p117 and How can I grow as a poet? on p119.) When responding to poetry writing, it is vital to focus upon the creative elements. Nothing is worse than when children are inhibited by the thought that the teacher might correct their spelling, grammar, punctuation etc. Because of this, you need to signal very clearly at each stage of the creative process that poetry, and creative writing time generally, is a special time when children should write freely without worrying about such issues.

As workshoppers, poets and teachers alike need to remember that children and adults function very differently. Adults fret over their work, procrastinate, want to perfect every line they create – polish it, draft it, work it until it is as good as they can make it, however long it may take.

Children, conversely, operate in the present tense. They want to write something 'now', then leave it and finish it there. They are not interested in writing a piece, leaving it to 'breathe' for a while, and then coming back to it at a later point to develop it further. Why should they? Gradually, a Year 5 or Year 6 class can be nurtured into seeing the benefits of 'the right word in the right place', the old chestnut 'less is more' and so on. Some pieces for 10- and 11-year-olds can be developed/polished, but not all of them.

Stage 7 - Publish

Although it is vital that children's writing is published in some form or another (see LET'S LIVE: Publishing children's poems on p16), not every piece will get finished off, and, as I said above, this is good. It is essential for children to have an incentive, purpose and motivation for writing, and publishing – be it in book form, on the school website or on a corridor display – will contribute towards children feeling that they are not just readers, but writers too.

Demonstrating the creative process

Envelope poems

When I go into classrooms to do workshops, I begin each session by showing the class my books. The most important book I show them is the Tintin book, 'The Black Island', as this is the book that turned me into a reader. And I wouldn't be a writer if I wasn't a reader. Children need to have the connections between reading and writing made explicit. Next, I show them an envelope – with doodles and jottings and notes and ideas all over it. One that might look something like the above illustration.

I then show the class a rough draft of one of my poems. Some children seem horrified and shocked. Horrified that my process is so messy, and perhaps shocked by the fact that, as if by some miracle, a poem pops straight out of my head and into a published book! They also seem stunned when I tell them each and every poem I write takes **at least** three months to write – changing the title, the words, the lines around, to find better ways to say things, to add new ideas, to take old ones out until I'm finally happy with it. Children need to see that there is a whole process involved and learn that every piece of writing is not written in an instant and will need some, if not considerable 'tweaking'. It's a good word, tweaking. Drafting isn't. It sounds very, very dull to a 9-, 10- or 11-year-old. As I said earlier, show your class the two versions of 'How To Build A Dragon' on p116.

Often, I'll encourage children to bring an old, used envelope into school the next day, an envelope with a little poem on it, one that the children can read and then later work on to develop into a full poem, if they wish. Or, you could put up a little display of some envelope poems. Children love doing this and it shows that writing can be about putting little thoughts down onto a scrap of paper like an envelope, a little thought that might grow into something bigger, or might be just a little bit of fun to be had every now and then. Why not try it?

Let's Write Poetry for a Reason

Across the curriculum - writing for a reason

This chapter, as with the rest of the book, actively seeks to encourage classes to move away from simply doing small modules of poetry, with the kind of Week 1 is cinquains, Week 2 is limericks approach – and to encourage teachers to use poetry dynamically and creatively to allow children to use simple but expressive poetic forms to celebrate and make sense of the subjects they are learning and experiencing.

I'm yet to be convinced that poetry modules work well, as it can so easily end up with children writing poems for the sake of writing poems, words for the sake of words. The most committed and spirited writing that I've seen is that outside of literacy, writing that stems from topic work and real experiences, which is exactly the kind of writing that this chapter sets out to explore and exploit. But, as far as I can see, poetry modules are most effective when poetry is already a regular feature in the classroom.

With poetry, as with maths and all forms of learning, a recursive approach is vital. If children only did fractions in Year 3 where would that lead them? I get both teachers and children saying to me, 'Oh we did haikus in Year 4.' As if to say we did that, let's do something else now. You can only be really good at haikus if you do them regularly. Likewise rhymes, kennings and all the other forms. Do people ever say to me 'Paragraphs? We did them in Year 2.' Of course not!

What can be better than immersing children in a subject, a theme or a topic, getting them really involved and fired up about pirates, dinosaurs, the body, the Ancient Egyptians or whatever and then asking them to capture that creative energy in the form of a rap, a shape poem, or a rhyme?

The range of poetry models provided here are to help you explore a variety of topics and curricular topics. But in no way are the topics/subject areas highlighted definitive or exhaustive – a KS1 teacher looking through the 'Kennings' section might be doing a topic on pirates and decide to use this form as a model and create with her class a pirate kenning.

Kennings do not necessarily have to be done within the context of a particular school theme or topic. You might decide

75

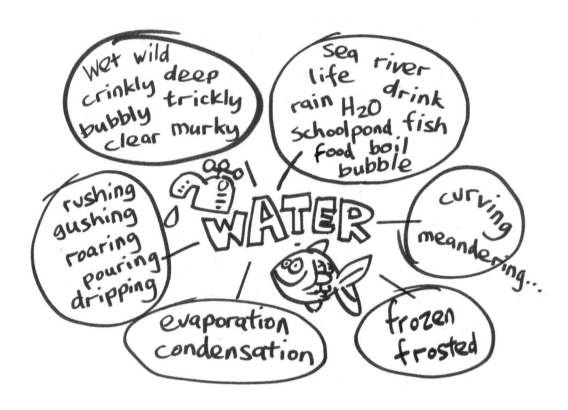

As you begin each topic why not put up a large piece of paper called 'Word Web', which can be a place for teacher and class alike to add words that might be useful when writing poems as you explore your topic.

for your class to write a kenning about the school's headteacher, a rap on Harry Potter or a tanka about the school pond. (All of which I've witnessed as I've visited schools around the UK.) Please feel free to take any aspect of the workshops that follow for your own creative uses.

Poems cover every topic under the sun, including the sun, the stars, the planets, science and everything beyond. As a poet I've been invited to run poetry workshops on Maths days, in Japanese weeks, in Love-A-Tree days, at Primary Science conferences, and many, many more.

The models of poetry that follow are rhymes, raps, kennings, syllabic verse

(cinquains, haikus and tankas), free verse, list poems, shape poems, acrostics/ alphabets. (But please do go back to the Poetry warm-ups and games that start on p63 as there are a number of activities there that might also prove useful when adopted and adapted for cross-curricular/topic work.)

Whatever form you are writing in, whatever topic is your focus, it is worth mentioning to the class that (as I've said earlier) poetry is based on repetition. Whether it's a rap or a shape poem or whatever, repetition is the fundamental ingredient, and it helps to know this. Repetition comes in many guises – as alliteration, assonance, rhyme, rhythm, as choruses, as listing. If children are stuck, ask them to see if they can repeat something they have already written in their poem, to give them a structure, a pattern. Enjoy!

Rhymes

Working with rhyme

Ask any Primary child what a poem is, and you can be certain the answer will be 'something that rhymes'. It's even the case with Years 5 and 6, who know well about other forms such as free verse and haikus by then. Why? Because children hear so much rhyme from birth, in the form of lullabies, nonsense rhymes, skipping rhymes, limericks and so on that they are conditioned by it. Also, coupled with rhythm, it's the element of poetry that many children most enjoy. Teachers and even poets often shy away from rhyme in workshops as it is difficult for children to do well, but however hard you try and move them away from it, the temptation will always be there.

So, what to do? Let them rhyme! I know what you're thinking – but children use 'lazy' rhymes and find it difficult to scan well. Okay, we'll start by letting them practise rhyming out of context. Let them think about rhymes as well as half-rhymes, let them count syllables and so on. All this will make them more proficient at writing rhyming poetry. There are some useful rhyme practices such as 'I've got a friend' on p78. You might want your class to do some of these before attempting any of the rhymes that follow – and that includes every year from Year 1 to Year 6.

A **rhyme scheme** tells you where the corresponding rhymes appear in a poem – and in which lines the rhymes appear. An AABB rhyme scheme informs you that the first two lines rhyme together, the third and fourth lines rhyme together and so on. An AABB rhyme scheme is also known as a **rhyming couplet**. These are the simplest and most common of rhyme schemes used in poetry writing in the Primary years. Here's an example:

> With these crayons I could draw (A)
>
> a crazy purple dinosaur. (A)
>
> An orange mouse with yellow cheese, (B)
>
> a big brown dog with big black fleas. (B)

The rhyming poems that follow in this section should give you pointers on how to use rhyming couplets to explore a theme.

The key issue with rhyming poetry is more the point of view from which you write the poem, what your 'spin' on the topic is. Take the Romans. You could write a simple rhyme about what a Roman soldier wore, in the first person, describing what he was wearing as he invaded Britain. Another poem might be 'What Did The Romans Do For Us?' and tell of all the things that Romans brought to Britain. In essence, it's not **what** you write about in a poem, it's **how** you write about it.

We've all seen children's rhyming poems that are full of 'random' and 'lazy' rhymes, something along the lines of:

> I went to the beach
> I sat on a peach
> I tried to teach

What can you say? Well, for a start, it rhymes well, but does it make sense? Of course not! Why not put up a big sign in the classroom that says:

> A LAZY RHYME IS A POETRY CRIME!

And that should get the point home. Ask the children to do a giant poster of 'A LAZY RHYME IS A POETRY CRIME!' They could even cover the poster with rhyming words, such as brain/train, new/few, show/know etc. – as well as half-rhymes: round/spout, cold/foal, shoe/boot.

Now, before we begin with some useful rhyme practices, here is a note on rhythm and some golden rules for rhyming.

A note on rhythm

Rhyming isn't the hardest element of writing a poem, rhythm is. And that's why writing a rhyming poem can be difficult to do well. To make a poem scan and flow well takes years of practice and not all professional poets can master it. Rhythm and scansion depend on many things:

- the words in a line

- the number of/combination of words in a line

- the number of syllables used

- the stresses, vowels and consonants in those words

But that's enough, for this is moving beyond KS2 expectations. Though the rule of thumb is: if it feels right, flows right, sounds right then the rhythm is working well.

One general, simple way to tell if the scansion is working is to count the syllables in a couplet. (The word 'poem' has two syllables; the word 'poetry' has three. Clap them out loud and you will see.) Ideally, each line will have a similar number of syllables.

> I'm a little alien - can't you see? (10)
> The grooviest guy in the galaxy! (10)

If you have one line that is nine syllables, and the next is five, you'll know you've got some tweaking to do.

The golden rule of rhythm is simple: keep going. Read your poem aloud. Get others to read it to you. Discuss how those words could flow better, whether it means reducing the number of words/syllables, changing the words altogether or simplifying the words that you have. Good luck!

Rhyme practices

So that children become more competent at both rhythm and rhyme, it is very useful to do fun, rhyming exercises such as the following ones using names of children and children's pets.

I've got a friend

I've got a friend
her name is Ruth
She loves to wiggle
her wobbly tooth

Golden Rules for Rhyming

- BE CAREFUL what rhymes you use. Try to avoid 'lazy' or 'random' rhymes. Remember – A LAZY RHYME IS A POETRY CRIME!

- Think of AS MANY RHYMES as you can before choosing the best one, the one that makes sense in your poem, and says what you want it to say.

- Go through THE ALPHABET looking for rhymes. So, if you want a rhyme for 'tree' you could put each letter of the alphabet at the start of the word to find a suitable rhyme – 'A/ee', 'B/ee', 'C/ee' and so on. Try initial clusters too – 'bl' 'br' 'ch' and so on. Also be aware that a rhyme for a word such as 'tree' might not end in 'ee' – and might be 'key' or 'sea' or 'me'.

- Do not be afraid to use HALF-RHYMES. Some children, even Infants, will automatically use half-rhymes, but others need more persuading. So, a half-rhyme for 'coat' would be 'bone' or 'cat'. You either keep the assonant sound – the 'oa' or keep the consonant sound – the 't'.

- If you can't think of a good rhyme, RE-PHRASE THE LINE or think of DIFFERENT WORDS altogether.

- To make sure the poem SCANS WELL, check that the lines are all of similar lengths. A good way to do this is to count the SYLLABLES. Look at this rhyming couplet: 'Why are we so afraid of the dark?/It doesn't bite and it doesn't bark.' The rhythm is tight, and this is partly due to the fact both lines have nine syllables.

- Ask someone to READ YOUR POEM OUT LOUD to you. Listen to the rhymes and the rhythm of the poem. See if it is working well or if it needs some tweaking.

- To use a RHYMING DICTIONARY or not? A great many teachers will disagree when I say that using a book during creative time is a big distraction, plus children need to get in to the habit of working out rhymes/re-jigging lines themselves.

- It could well be that your poem DOESN'T WANT TO RHYME. Let it be free verse if it wants to. Or even dip in and out of rhyme, though one thing is certain – if you start a poem with rhyme, you have to continue, as once the ear hears rhyme it wants to hear more.

Note that the rhyme scheme in 'Friends' is such that the rhymes fall at the end of lines 2 and 4.

Now try a name with two syllables.

> I've got a friend
> her name is Mia
> I always laugh
> whenever she's near!

Upper KS2 children could try half-rhymes (see the note on half-rhymes in the Golden Rules for Rhyming on p79), as in 'Kim' and vio-'lin':

> I've got a friend
> her name is Kim
> she loves to play
> the violin.

Pets

> My dog is big
> my dog is brown
> he likes to chase
> around the town.

This is another very simple but fun way of getting children to work on rhymes out of context before they embark on something more ambitious. Again, make sure that the lines are all of similar length.

And now, with a half-rhyme, 'white' and 'hide':

> My cat is small
> my cat is white
> and after dark
> he'll go and hide.

If children choose a two syllable pet, such as hamster (or even three or four) the line would need to be abbreviated:

> My hamster's cute
> my hamster's ...

And so on.

Having done some simple rhyme practices, here are a few examples of rhymes that make good structures for use in the classroom.

Emotional animal rhymes

Animal-based topics (or even aspects of the natural world, such as rainforests) are prevalent in all Primary schools. Nothing could be simpler than this fun structure, and it is suitable for Foundation to Year 6. First read this verse of 'Happy Poem':

> Happy as a rainbow, happy as a bee (A)
> happy as a dolphin, splashing in the sea. (A)

This is a rhyming couplet, but it is just as easy to write it as a quatrain, and easier for a young child to read too:

> Happy as a rainbow,
> happy as a bee
> happy as a dolphin,
> splashing in the sea.

This way, the rhymes fall at the end of lines 2 and 4.

Ask the class to think of another animal that might be 'happy'. You could ask for an animal that either alliterates with 'happy' or has a double 'p' in it. Syllables play a big part in this poem so even with Year 1 you will need to get them clapping syllables. (See LET'S LEARN POETRY: Syllables on p18). Inform the class that you are looking for an animal that always seems happy, a two-clap animal, maybe one that begins with an 'h'. Responses might be 'hippo', 'monkey', 'bunny'. All these will do fine. So let's say, we have:

> Happy as a hippo.

For the next line, you need a one-clap animal. Children might give you all kinds of animals but now you will want one that will rhyme with another animal, so you need something like bat/cat/rat or dog/hog/frog or seal/eel. Say you pick 'dog'. You now need an adjective to describe the dog, and children might give you 'yappy', 'crazy', 'noisy – and you might choose to do:

> Happy as a hippo
> yappy as a dog.

And if you do, you can point out that 'happy' and 'yappy' also rhyme.

From here you could jump to line four – and put in say, 'jumpy as a frog' and then look for another animal with two syllables – again, with an adjective to match, and the class might give you 'cheetah' and then 'speedy'. So, very quickly, we have a first verse:

> Happy as a hippo
> yappy as a dog
> speedy as a cheetah
> jumpy as a frog.

It's the same principle with the other verses. You might decide that your class does just one verse each or even a whole poem, say of three or four verses. It is good if the final verse can end on a conclusive, rounding-off note, e.g.

> Graceful as an eagle
> soaring through the sky
> these were the animals
> say 'goodbye!'

On the following page there is a version of this poem written with two Infant classes. Note the extra counting section to the poem at the end (which I added for this version). You could adopt this and adapt it for your own class poem if you wish – but you will need to finish with 'busy as a bee' (or 'itchy as a flea')/'how many animals can we see?' in order to start off the counting sequence that follows.

List-repetition poems

There are a number of types of list poems. One type is literally a 'list' of things in a simple non-rhyming list, such as Ian McMillan's modern classic 'Ten Things Found in a Wizard's Pocket'. Another is to have a list within a rhyming structure; there is an example, 'Night Soup' on p51. Why not try your own version? Or even do a 'Day Soup' or 'Winter Soup', 'Holiday Soup' or 'Summer Soup'?

The other type, another rhyming list poem, doesn't have an official name, but I call them 'list-repetition poems'. These repeat the key word of the piece. They are fun, simple, and perfect for Foundation and KS1, and great for writing and chanting out loud. Giles Andrae and Nick Sharrat's ever popular picture book 'Pants' is written in this form, as is my 'Bears, Bears, Bears' poem, of which the first two verses are:

How Do Animals Feel?

Happy as a hippo
hairy as a dog
hungry as a lion
hoppy as a frog

Splashy as a dolphin
flappy as a bat
bouncy as a rabbit
scratchy as a cat

Spikey as a hedgehog
busy as a bee…
how many animals
can you see?

One for the hippo
two for the dog
three for the lion
four for the frog
five for the dolphin
six for the bat
seven for the rabbit
eight for the cat
nine for the hedgehog
ten for the bee.
TEN wild animals we can see!

Written by the Year 1 classes of All Saints CE Primary School, Didcot with James Carter on National Poetry Day 2011

Grizzly bears
honey bears
itchy titchy funny bears

Cheeky chappy
chubby bears
bears
bears
bears!

This poetic form can be done within all kinds of topics, just a few of which are listed below.

Transport is a popular boy-centred topic at KS1. Begin by choosing the specific subject, say boats. Find some adjectives to describe a boat, and even words associated with a boat – big/long/blue/green/wide/sea/wave/port.

And then mix some of these together:

Green boats, grey boats
bobbing on the waves boats
travelling far away boats
boats, boats, boats!

Weather is another perennial topic. Here is one verse of a snow list poem. Try wind, rain, mist, sun and so on.

Big snow, thick snow
snow you could lick snow,
white snow, bright snow
snow, snow, snow!

Minibeasts has to be **the** topic for KS1/Foundation, and perfect for rhymes. Tony Mitton has written his own list-repetition bugs poem. It's a great poem in itself, and a perfect model for writing. It's in 'The Works' (the first one, the red one, in nearly every Primary school library.) Here's my own adapted version, with a little added chorus:

Wriggly bugs
sticky bugs
bugs that feel so tickly bugs.
creepy bugs
leafy bugs
Bugs, Bugs, Bugs!

Very simple, very achievable. Write a list of different minibeasts on the board. Then brainstorm adjectives to describe all the minibeasts. Now, find adjectives that work well together, words that alliterate, rhyme or have the same number of syllables.

Here is another list-form, this time with the subject of the poem at the start of each line:

Caterpillar - creep and crawl
caterpillar - up the wall
caterpillar - ten feet tall!

Try a spider, ladybird, butterfly or a different bug.

However, if you lose rhyme altogether, and focus on imagery, you could achieve a free verse, list poem, along the lines of:

Moths that flicker like autumn leaves.

Fireflies that shine like scribbled gold.

Ants as strong as marching armies.

Dragonflies that zip like rockets.

Children so enjoy rhyme, but without it, there is even more freedom to be creative, and children need experience of both rhyming and non-rhyming forms.

Counting animals

The following poem could be used in a topic on either animals or the senses (hearing):

Can You Hear...

ONE the growl of the grizzly bear
TWO the stomp of the Mad March hare
THREE the whine of the hungry cat
FOUR the squeak of the speedy bat
FIVE the caw of the crow in flight
SIX the bark of the fox at night
SEVEN the squawk of the parrot's cry
EIGHT the zip of the humble fly
NINE the grunt of a pig in a pen
TEN let's hear them all again...

As a class, brainstorm lists of animals and the different sounds they make. Because most of the rhymes are types of animals, these will need to be single syllable animals. You could even begin by finding animal names that rhyme first of all: frog/dog/hog, cat/rat/bat, eel/seal, quail/whale, bee/flea and so on.

Odes

Traditionally odes were romantic ballads to be taken seriously. Nowadays, more often than not, odes are tongue-in-cheek. People write odes to their pets, their heroes, their guitar (guilty!), all kinds. What makes an ode fun is that you celebrate all the different positive qualities about a subject.

And what makes an ode unique is that it will mainly be written in the second person, as you are addressing it to a 'you'.

This is the opening verse of a romantic ode:

> You are the light
> that starts my day
> that ups and burns
> the night away.

Let's shift this into a different gear with a pirate ode, for pirates are an increasingly popular topic at both KS1 and KS2.

> You are the thief
> that ruled the waves
> with sword held high
> So wild, so brave.

Why not try an ode to a tree/Henry VIII/ Queen Victoria/the sun/the ocean?

Raps

Although raps come from American street culture and are an integral part of the hip hop genre, rap poems are, in the main, fun, funky and highly appropriate for Primary schools. Try one of Tony Mitton's wonderful rap books published by Orchard.

Raps are simply rhyming poems with a straightforward AABB (rhyming couplet) rhyme scheme with a bit of added attitude! But this doesn't mean to say that they can't deal with serious topics, it's just that they are delivered in a modern, fun way.

Rap poems are great for both KS1 and KS2. Some brave teachers might choose to write and scribe a rap with a class on the board. In general, raps are written individually or in small groups by Years 5 and 6 as they demand a lot of a young writer. Until then, they make for ideal performance poems for Years 2, 3 and 4.

As with all rhyming poems, it's a question of keeping to a tight rhythm and using good rhymes – see the Golden Rules for Rhyming on p79 and A note on rhythm on p78.

Topics

Whatever topic you may pick for a rap, you will need two things: a) a subject brainstorm, so you know what you want to discuss as well as what language you may wish to use, and b) a good, solid introduction.

Say you decide to rap about a **rainforest**:

> Now, yo there, dudes, you listen up good
>
> Cos we're going to take you through da wood
>
> a tour of magic and mystery
>
> from the forest floor to the canopy
>
> with exotic things for you to see...

Anatomical Rap

Hey everybody, listen to me
and my anatomical a–zee
the human biology hip hop show
now here we go, from head to toe...

The cranium keeps the brain in place
two eyes shine inside the face
the teeth are there to munch and crunch
saliva helps digest your lunch

CHORUS: Everything you need to know
in this human hip hop show!

The nose breathes in, the lungs expand
the heart pumps blood – around and around
then the kidneys, liver, spleen
filter blood – to keep it clean.
CHORUS

The tummy, intestines, process food
we'll say no more – the rest is rude!
CHORUS

What will support, protect and grow
the skeleton – don't you know!
Eat a balanced diet, take care of your health
but most of all, look after yourself!

Year 4 class, Telferscot Primary School (with James Carter)

Or even the **Victorians**:

Yo, fancy being historians?

And learning about the Victorians?

Now check these out, these celebrities:

Dickens, yes, and the three Brontes...

Darwin, Gladstone and Brunel

and Alexander Graham Bell...

Other great topics to rap with – Vikings, Celts, Ancient Greeks, Ancient Egyptians, Tudors and Henry VIII, minibeasts, recycling and sports to name but a few.

Story retellings using rap

Read the fairy tale rap 'Porky Pies!' on p61.

Raps are probably the most fun you can have with performance poetry. They are great for slightly irreverent, mischievous retellings of famous stories – from fairy and folk tales, to Greek myths, Aesop's fables, all kinds. Roald Dahl's 'Revolting Rhymes' were proto-raps, and would be a good starting point for children hearing stories retold in mischievous rhyming couplets!

Rap work is ideally done in mixed ability groups. Some children take to raps and rhyming very easily, others simply don't have a feel for it, or struggle with rhythm and rhyme and need to be guided by others.

A workshop should begin with perhaps one or two raps being read aloud, with the teacher highlighting the rhythm and the rhymes, the humour and the spin on the original story. From there, these top tips could be put on the board as pointers.

Top tips for raps

Introduction – The class will need to be given some kind of opening first, to make sure they have a solid rhythmic foundation to open up with, say a generic:

> Everybody in da hood, now listen, yo –
>
> Here comes a tale that you might just know
>
> It's all about...

Or, as in a hip hop style, the rappers can include their names – or aspects of their names. For instance, there might be two girls called Emily and Molly, a pair of girls writing together, and they could begin with:

> Everybody in da room, listen yo!
> Here's a rap from Em and Mo...

Tell half the story – Children do not need to tell the whole story. If they are doing the fairy tale Little Red Riding Hood, they could begin when Red is knocking on her granny's door, or with Cinderella, with the heroin arriving at the ball.

Good rhymes/half-rhymes – One reason to do raps is to improve children's rhyming skills (see Golden Rules for Rhyming on p79). Children need to be reminded to use good rhymes and even half-rhymes, and also keep the rhythm flowing well. It may help, if they are doing fairy tales to

abbreviate names such as Rapunzel (to Rap), Cinderella (to Cindy or Little Miss C), Rumpelstiltskin (to Rumpie), Hansel and Gretel (to H and G) and so on, as they sound more modern and are easier for rhythm and rhyme.

A bit of bling! Raps need attitude. Brainstorm some modern, colloquial 'street' words they could use in their raps to inject some attitude – like yo, bling, wossup, da hood, whatever, dude, bruv, sis – and of course, innit!

Genres/modes to rap with – fairy tales, fables, myths, Greek myths, legends, novels (try Roald Dahl's 'Matilda', Jacqueline Wilson's 'Tracy Beaker' or J. K. Rowling's 'Harry Potter').

Kennings

Alongside raps, kennings are arguably the most fun and exciting of all poems for both KS1 and KS2 children to write as well as perform. Kennings can captivate even the most reluctant writers. One seemingly demotivated post-SATS Year 6 class I visited a while ago refused to go out to break because they wanted to finish off the kennings they were writing. Result!

Each two-word line of a kenning brings together two different elements (as in 'mighty-biter' and 'fierce-fighter' in 'What Was I?' on the next page) and, more often than not, a noun-noun, a noun-verb or an adjective-verb. Together, the two words create a metaphor, and ultimately, throughout a kenning poem, a full image of its subject, often an animal. Having two words in each line sets up a regular, rolling rhythm. Read the kenning 'What Was I?' aloud. How does it read?

What Was I?

A...

long-goner
super-stomper

swamp-swimmer
death-bringer

head-banger
jaw-snapper

teeth-gnasher
bone-basher

mighty-biter
fierce-fighter

tiny-brainer
comet-hater

past-dweller
fossil-fella

The biggest
ever carnivore,
I was of course...
a dinosaur!

**James Carter with the
Infant class, Dorchester
St Birinus CE Primary School,
Dorchester on Thames**

Most commonly, a kenning poem will have up to twelve or so lines, and they do not have to rhyme. And although the second word has an 'er' sound it can be spelt with an 'or', 'a' or 'ure' – as in the word 'fella' below. One strict rule is that kennings can't include the name of the subject that is being addressed. So, in a dog kenning for instance, you could not even include the lines 'puppy-producer' or 'dog-food eater'.

To reinforce the basic rules in a kenning workshop, it is good every now and then to ask the class: What are these poems called? Kennings! How many words per line? Two! The second word ends in what sound? -er!

Warm up – As a fun warm-up, ask the class in pairs to devise their own one-line animal kennings. First, put these on the board as examples: 'bone-burier' (dog), 'sofa-scratcher' (cat), 'wave-maker' (whale) and 'back-scratcher' (hedgehog).

Kennings about animals – Pick an animal. Brainstorm with the class what that animal does. Put all the key words, especially verbs, on the board too. Now write out the structure below (What am I? -lover/-hater etc.) on the board. Now, slowly work through this list and fill in the gaps. It does not have to be done in order.

If you were to brainstorm words for a dog kenning, you might come up with words such as 'chaser' and 'racer', which could become 'squirrel-chaser' and 'rapid-racer'.

With KS2 classes – especially Years 4, 5 and 6 – I usually insist that they do a kenning as a riddle, as it is great fun trying to guess what animal it is. It also encourages children to consider their chosen animal more creatively, as they can't always put down the first thought they come up with. Because of this I tend to discourage lines like 'banana-eater' for monkey or 'bone-lover' for dog. And, as I said earlier, you can't mention what type of animal it is in the poem, and it is best to be as cryptic as possible.

What Is It?

............-lover
............-hater
............-giver
............-taker
............-eater
............-maker
............-creature
............-dweller
............-fella

So, if you were to do a dog, it could become:

owner-lover
noise-hater
pleasure-giver
time-taker

and so on. Now the class can begin to write their own kennings, copying down the whole template structure. With older and more able groups, it is good to encourage children to use alliterative kennings where possible (such as 'fierce-fella', 'mess-maker'), as this adds extra texture to the poem. However, this could also be a drafting device: going back to the kenning in a second or third session, putting alliteration into lines, for example, turning 'furniture-wrecker' into 'sofa-scratcher'. And also, internal rhymes – so 'flesh-eater' could become 'meat-eater'.

Children do not have to stick to all of the '-giver'/'-taker' cue words and might want to add kenning lines of their own.

Even if they write more than 12 lines, ask the class to edit it down to 12. (This work is ideally done in a second or third sitting.) They might even wish to change the order of the lines to get a better flow. When the 12 lines are completed, they can add this coda verse or even think of their own version:

Of all the ... (mammals/predators/pets)

I'm the best!

I'm a ... (name your animal here)

Had you guessed?

Kennings with other topics/themes/subjects – The dinosaur kenning 'What Was I?' was written as a direct request from an Infant teacher to write a poem with her class about their current topic, dinosaurs. But kennings can be used in most class topics (or aspects of) and can act as list poems or summaries of facts and knowledge covered during a topic. For instance, the Ancient Egyptians become 'desert-dwellers', 'pyramid-producers', 'mummy-makers', 'hieroglyphic-scribers', 'cat-lovers', 'Nile-navigators' and so on. The Infant class at Lewknor Primary School made a papier mâché dragon with a kenning beneath it. El Limonar International School in Murcia, Spain, get their Year 3 classes to write a Harry Potter kenning every year. Kintbury St Mary's Year 5 class even wrote a kenning about their headteacher.

Possibly, unlike any other form of poetry, kennings allow you to view your chosen topic from many different and disparate angles in very few words. Though only recommended as an optional form for Primary schools, kennings can be and regularly are produced in schools from Year 3 across to Year 6, and even into Secondary in Years 7 and 8.

Performance – Kennings are perfect for poetry performances and assemblies. Perhaps encourage six or so members of your class to read them out in the next assembly. It also works well if pairs read together, swopping lines and even adding actions, which really brings the kenning to life. Ask them to read the final rhyming stanza, but leave out the name of the subject, and from there they can ask members of the class/school to guess what their subject is.

Syllabic poems: cinquains, haikus and tankas

KS2 children take so readily to syllabic poetry. They love the whole process of counting syllables, but, and here's the rub, they can get too carried away with the counting and forget that the words are the most important aspect of these poems. The point is that syllabic poems have to say and mean something – they're not just random words fulfilling set patterns of numbers.

Syllabic poetry is wonderful for simple but striking imagery, for honing in on the micro of language, for selecting and rejecting words and expressing a great deal with so little. This is a good discipline for children's writing as a whole, and ideally, children would do syllabic poetry most terms from Year 4 onwards.

Cinquains are five-line poems, with ascending numbers of syllables per lines 2/4/6/8 then finishing on 2. This allows the poet to build up a series of images or statements about its subject.

Cinquains can be written as riddles, so only the last line reveals the identity of the subject.

> A fire. (2)
> An inferno. (4)
> A blazing, gazing eye. (6)
> And one golden, open oven... (8)
> The sun. (2)

The place to start is by brainstorming a topic on the board. If you were doing a river, you could ask the questions: 'What is a river like?' 'What does it look like from above?' 'How does it move?' 'Where does it go?' 'Where has it been?' 'What does it see along the way?' Responses to these could then be used as raw material for the poem.

Below is a cinquain created in a class writing session to celebrate the Diamond Jubilee:

Cinquains

Sealions
(Whipsnade Zoo, summer 2011)

On land:
clumsy as clowns,
though once in the water:
graceful as angels, as eagles
in air.

> The Queen
> sovereign, proud
> speaking, waving, smiling.
> Served our country for 60 years
> leader
>
> Harry Salmon, Year 4,
> Leehurst Swan School, Salisbury

Cinquain topics to consider – the ocean, the sky, a shadow, the moon, space, water and so on.

Haikus

> Ever seeking shade.
> Scitters over blazing sand:
> One lime green lizard.

Haikus are of Japanese origin, from the 17th century. Traditionally, haikus focus on a specific time and place and represent the natural world. Haikus quite frequently and simply bear the title 'Haiku'. The important thing to remember is that the haiku is a mini-snapshot in words, a little moment frozen in time. Haikus have just three lines and seventeen syllables in total – the first line has five syllables, the second has seven and the third has five:

Tiger Haiku

Through moonlit jungle (5)
strolling, stalking then striking: (7)
time to feast on flesh. (5)

Because of the focus on nature, haikus are ideal for writing about the seasons, minibeasts, all aspects of nature, as well as trips to zoos, farms, arboretums and aquariums.

Top tips for animal haikus

Brainstorm key words – Once you have decided on a subject e.g. an animal, ideally one that you know something about, first write down as many words as you can to describe the creature. Now think of as many words as you can that describe how the creature moves. Now write down 'What is the animal doing?' 'What is the time of day?' 'Where is it taking place?' 'What will happen next?' and work through these. You will now have far more material than you need. Use the three lines to portray your chosen animal, and perhaps each line could focus on a different aspect of your topic, perhaps the place/the time of day/what is happening. You do not even have to do the lines in order.

Focus on the words, not the numbers – The number of syllables are important, but more so are the words, and the way that you use those words.

Keep the syllable count to 5/7/5 – Try and avoid using adverbs, instead use an expressive verb. Instead of an animal that 'ran quickly' try 'dashed' or 'darted' or 'sprinted' or 'sped' or 'leapt'.

Short words can be cut – Words such as 'the' or 'a' or 'an' or even at times 'and' can be left out so long as it is still grammatical and makes sense.

You do not have to name the animal – As you have so few words, it can be a waste of syllables to name the creature in the poem, so, if you wish, only mention it in the title. (If you do this, teachers can then ask the children to read out their haikus – without the titles – so the rest of the class has to listen closely for clues as to what the animal might be.)

Show don't tell – Use colour, texture, the five senses, anything to depict that place and time and bring the creature and its surroundings to life. Also, try to avoid bland phrases or clichés like 'hunting/searching for its prey'. Most animals do this anyway.

Senryus

For a very different form of haiku, try one based upon a fable or fairy tale. This form of haiku is called a senryu and still has the same syllables, but is based on people/narrative rather than the natural world. It does not have to rhyme, like the example below, but simply has to sum up or give an insight to an aspect of the story.

Hare & Tortoise Senryu

Outcome curious:
tortoise was victorious.
Hare was furious!

Tankas

A tanka is for more experienced young writers, as it is an extension of the haiku, with two extra lines of seven syllables: 5/7/5/7/7. Also tankas, because they have two more lines than haikus, allow the writer to go into a little more detail.

Tanka: Monkey
(Whipsnade Zoo, summer 2011)

After feeding time, (5)
monkey spots a stray apple (7)
bobbing on the pond - (5)
armed with a long branch he tries (7)
but fails to reach the fruit. Ahh! (7)

Good haiku/tanka topics – aspects of the countryside (trees, leaves, animals, nocturnal creatures, the seasons, birds, fruit), farms, zoos, arboretums as well as space.

Free verse

What's the antidote to too much rhyming? Free verse. What's the best medium for children to express their ideas, their thoughts and feelings, to explore their memories and celebrate aspects of their lives? Free verse. What's a flexible and creative medium, good for developing prose skills, imagery, metaphors, similes, as well as fresh and exciting language? Yes, of course, free verse!

More so than any other children's writer, Michael Rosen has shown that free verse is a wonderful medium for writing about your own life, your reflections. Rosen in turn was influenced by free verse pioneers, American writers like Carl Sandburg, William Carlos Williams and ee cummings.

In fact, free verse is a close sibling to prose, but often the main differences are a) its brevity and b) it will be broken up into lines and verses rather than sentences and paragraphs. Free verse has a quiet, subtle rhythm, akin to prose, but often the language will be slightly more musical, from the repetition of sounds in alliteration and assonance, and occasionally will even employ rhymes.

As simple as it looks, or can look on the page, children can struggle initially with free verse as they do not know how to set it out. Well, they need to practise! To this end, choose an opening sentence from a classic novel and make it look like a free verse poem.

Take this opening line from Kenneth Grahame's 'The Wind in the Willows': 'The mole had been working very hard all the morning, spring-cleaning his little home.' When laid out as free verse, this could end up looking like this, with the chapter title included as well:

The River Bank

The mole
    had been
        working

very hard
    all the morning

Spring-cleaning
    his little home.

This is just one of many ways it could be laid out. I decided, as there were so few words, to 'step' the lines, and also because it would slow the reader down. I also removed the comma because it was unnecessary, as now, in the form of a poem, and with line breaks, the piece punctuates itself.

The hardest thing for children is to work out where to put the line and verse breaks, as there are no set rules, but the more that children write free verse, the more confident they will feel about making such decisions. Where you break the lines and verses will affect the look, feel and meaning of the poem. Doing an exercise such as this – taking a sentence of prose and making it look like free verse – will certainly help. Moreover, the more free verse children read on a regular basis, or see on displays around the classroom, the more it will feed into their writing. Why not try a display of poems by Michael Rosen, Brian Moses, ee cummings or William Carlos Williams – or some of the free verse poems in this book, say 'Heaven' p53, 'Talking Teeth' p56, 'We are Learning To... & What I'm Looking For' p45, 'Playgrounds' p50 and 'The Story of Water' p60.

When you lay out a piece like this, you are more aware of the sounds, music and textures of the words and lines. Note the words 'mole' and 'home'. These are half-rhymes, as are 'had' and 'hard'. Note the assonance of 'all' and the first syllable of 'mor-ning'. Also, note that there are three words in this short sentence that end in 'ing'. Coincidence? No, none of this is. Writers instinctively write in a musical way, and Grahame was himself a poet, used to putting words together that chime well. Neither you nor the children in your class need to analyse prose to this degree, but there is no harm in pointing it out occasionally!

Some free verse, like Michael Rosen's, is very colloquial, and uses everyday language. Other free verse can be more traditionally 'poetic' and uses rich, expressive language such as alliteration, assonance and repetition and will employ metaphor and imagery. Compare the free verse poems 'Night Car Journey' p95, 'Playgrounds' p50 and 'The Story of Water' p60 and notice the differences in the use of language and the overall effect.

Some teachers dismiss free verse as too 'anything goes'. Well, my response is that though it may seem free and unstructured at a glance, actually, for me, the opposite is the case. Free verse is often well crafted and subtly but tightly structured. Repeat readings of free verse poems will reveal this to be true – hopefully!

Free verse can be used to explore literally any topic in Primary schools – from water to Celts, from transport to Victorians. The key issue, however, is to find the voice and a structure within free verse to suit the topic at hand.

What Stars Are

Stars
are not
the shards of glass
smashed by the gods in anger.

Neither
are they the sparkling souls
of intergalactic travellers.

They're not even
the blinking eyes
of invisible skywatchers.

No.

Stars
  are
    Stars.

The
dying embers
of ancient fires
that will never know how
they dazzle and delight
us with the final
flickers of their
lives.

James Carter (Journey to the Centre of My Brain, Macmillan Children's Books)

Free verse poems about space

'What Stars Are' is a simple free verse poem that, in the first half, employs colourful imagery to evoke its subject. The second half explains the science behind the phenomenon of stars. This poem works as a useful model for children's own writing about many aspects of space, or indeed, the natural world.

This workshop is ideal for Years 5 and 6. It is useful for children exploring imagery and more decorative language, and to go beyond cliché.

First step – Read the poem through several times. Ask children to comment on the words, the structure of the poem, and what it says to them.

Second step – Choose a space-related topic: it could be black holes, time, shooting stars, the Milky Way, the universe, the moon, the planets. For this example, we'll pick the sun. Brainstorm words and ideas associated with the sun. What is the sun? What does it remind you of? What would it look like close up? What is it made of? Why does it exist? Where is it? When and how did it begin? Keep these ideas and write on the board the opening line below. Note how the title runs into the first line:

The Sun
  is not
    what it seems...

Then write a series of four or so 'Not the...' listing-style of opening phrases down the left-hand side. Try and find metaphoric, image-led phrases that might fit, e.g.:

Not the burning soul
                  of a fiery phoenix
Not the gazing eye
                  of a mighty cyclops

If children wish to find their own structure/opening, let them. The second half of the poem could become scientific, as the poem 'What Stars Are' does, or alternatively include some philosophical ideas, say a reflection on how the sun shapes, controls and informs our lives.

Children often default to using clichés like 'the moon is not made of cheese' or 'the Milky Way/Mars is not a chocolate bar', so it might help to dissuade them from such lines from the outset. I generally ban aliens and food analogies from this workshop, as I want to hear something new and exciting.

Free verse poems about memory

Once children are comfortable with writing free verse (ideally in Year 4 and above), a memory poem, such as 'Night Car Journey', should be straightforward to write. However, it's often a case of 'less is more' with this form of poem. For instance, there are many details that are left out of 'Night Car Journey' – such as who else is in the car, who is driving, why is the journey being made and so on. What this very simple poem seeks to do is to hone in on a brief moment in time, and word it as succinctly as possible. The poem is in the present tense, which makes it more immediate and atmospheric.

Compare 'Night Car Journey' with the free verse poem 'WALT & WILF' on p45. You will see that although this other poem

is also in the present tense, it contains dialogue and humour. Also look at the poem 'Talking Teeth' on p56. Another poem based on real-life experience, it is written in the present tense, and is very close to prose, and is even written in practically one paragraph of text.

For this workshop, children will need to choose a memory of their own – just a short moment, or an aspect of an event. Children could begin by brainstorming what took place/the time of day/who was present/where it took place/how it

Night Car Journey

I wake up
sitting in the back seat
not quite sure
if it's real or a dream

and I look up
out through the darkness
out through the silence
to an infinite sky

and the moon bobs
in and out of treetops
turning the world
a ghostly blue

and my eyes
are heavy now
my eyes
are heavy now
my

**James Carter
(Cars, Stars, Electric
Guitars, Walker Books)**

occurred/any conversation there might have been. Having mulled over the event for a few minutes or so, they could begin writing. They could also write in the present tense, and begin 'I'm...' and find an appropriate verb to follow on with say, 'talking', 'watching', 'listening', 'eating' or whatever fits with the memory. You could deliberately limit the writing by asking children to produce no more than a page, and this will mean that their writing will be disciplined and focused. Once they have done a first draft, the piece could be left for a day or two, and then returned to with a view to shortening the piece and making it as dynamic as possible – losing unnecessary dialogue or descriptions. For further editing tips, please refer to LET'S RESPOND TO POETRY: Poetry checklist on p117.

Children can be encouraged to use the five senses to bring their memory fully to life – with sights, sounds, smells, tastes, textures and so on. If children can't remember precise details, encourage them to improvise and be creative here. Autobiographical material, be it prose or verse, is never wholly 100% accurate to an original event. Also, the maxim 'Don't let the truth get in the way of a good story' might encourage young poets to let a little fiction creep into their memory poems. Furthermore, free verse memory poems could be used to explore specific topics covered in PSHE and circle time discussions – such as 'My first day at...', 'A time when I helped a friend', 'Feeling lonely in the playground' and so on – see Using free verse in PHSE: gifts on p99.

Other free verse topic starting points – daydreams, conversations, the time I told a fib, the best/worst time ever, the not-so-secret secret, the day that went from bad to worse, feeling like an outsider, my earliest memory, a dream come true, an embarrassing moment. It is impossible to list all the areas that free verse would be

good for, but I would argue that it could be useful in literally any topic.

Free verse – First-person poems in historical/mythological settings

This form of free verse will allow Upper Key Stage 2 classes to write about certain historical periods from a first person viewpoint. It will encourage children to imagine what it would have been like to live in a certain place at a certain time.

These outlines are starting points, and teachers may wish to adapt or embellish these according to their own needs and topics.

Victorians – Write a first-person poem in the voice of a child labourer, walking to work through the streets of London. What would they see? Who would they encounter? How would they feel about where they are going? You could open with something along the lines of the example below, perhaps opening each verse with a verb, I walk/I work/I ...

I wait
    for the bells to ring.

I wake
    before the night has gone.

I walk
    the drab and shabby streets.

I work...

Greeks – Write a first-person poem in the voice of a Greek soldier waiting inside the wooden horse before the attack on the city of Troy. What would it be like inside the horse in that hot climate? Would there be any light? What would they eat? How would the soldiers feel stuck inside there? Perhaps you could use 'We wait.' as the opening line to some of the verses as here:

> We wait.
>   Here in the horse
>   in the heat.
>
> Stifled, silent, still.
>
> We wait…

World War II – Although the Second World War is generally better served by prose, the air raids are an opportunity for atmospheric and onomatopoeic free verse. Try this opening:

> Another night
>   huddled together
>   in the shelter
>
> Another night
>   of darkness
>   and the sounds above…

Writing free verse poems about visits and school trips

As I've said elsewhere in this book, generally speaking, the best writing from children will stem from real experiences. Clearly, children will not have much time to sit around and write poems during a school trip – be it a one-day visit or even a residential trip, but they will have opportunities afterwards. As a visitor, I don't usually have the luxury to go on trips with children and then rework those experiences into crafted language, but what follows is a workshop that I did in my daughter's Year 5 and 6 class. The teacher asked me to come in and get the class writing free verse poems based on their residential trip to Woodlands, and in particular, the visit to the caves.

The class teacher primed the class the whole week before by looking at metaphors and similes. See LET'S PLAY: 'Have you seen my dragon?' and 'Super similes' both on p68.

To open the workshop, I read a couple of free verse poems, including 'Night Car Journey' (p93), explaining that I wanted them to write their own free verse pieces, also in the present tense – to make it more immediate and atmospheric. I explained that 'atmosphere' in writing gives the reader the experience of 'how it feels to be in a certain place at a certain time'.

I stressed the need to 'show' and not 'tell', saying they could 'tell' me that they were 'scared', but only if they 'showed' me that they were scared, for example, a phrase such as 'my heart beat, my clammy hands shook, my teeth chattered'. I also encouraged them to use the five senses, asking them to tell me what the rocks felt like, how cold it was, what they could hear, what the cave smelled like and so on.

First, I asked the class to brainstorm everything and anything they could remember about the experience, from which I received a range of random thoughts and ideas:

> cold/dark/inky black/black hole/ smelly like fish/excited but scared/cramped like a cellar or prison

Words that I felt were most powerful and expressive I collected in a communal brainstorm on the board.

I suggested that perhaps their poems could be their journeys into, through and out of the cave. I suggested that the first word of the poem (and perhaps every subsequent line or verse) should be 'I'm' so that they would a) have a starting point and a simple structure, and b) write in the present continuous tense. I asked the class for a good word to follow 'I'm' and one girl offered 'stepping', from which I improvised a stepped first line from their brainstorms:

Title... (to be written!)

I'm stepping
　　into this cellar
　　　　this prison
　　　　　　of inky blackness

I'm...

As a final note, I encouraged the class to exaggerate, to make the event more dramatic, and to not necessarily stick to the facts. Also, I quoted an author who had recently visited the school, Alan Durant, who believes that as a writer you do not have to be bound by the real events, and that you can 'let the fiction in'.

The poems that follow were written in a couple of sittings, and these are extracts of extended pieces.

extracts from
The Black Hole

I'm stepping into the mouth of the ferocious beast

Walking into the prison of inky blackness

Cold air wrapping me like a tornado

I'm an ant crawling on the back of a bumpy dragon

My voice booming everywhere as I speak

The smell of the diagusting odour going through my nose

I'm a fish swimming in the sea as cold as snow

I'm panicking if I would ever get out of the water...

Sithara Gunarajah,
Year 6, South Moreton
Primary School

extracts from

Dragon's Cave

I turn and whisper 'see you soon, daylight'.
Then I'm stepping into darkness.
This damp and rocky place.
We switch on our lights and see the jagged rocks.

Dragon claws coming round the corner.
The Dragon roars.
His flames come rushing round the corner.
I'm really scared.

Phew.
It was only the gushing of cold water.
It was only the light from head torches from another group.

We crawl under the rocks of muddy and sandy water,
Feeling the rough sand.

It smells like old wellies.
Then we turn off our lights.
It's as black as a Jaguar's fur.
It's as black as a Witch's cat...

Finn Walshe, Year 5, South Moreton
Primary School

These are both very vivid pieces, redolent and full of atmosphere. The first is akin to a cumulative list of responses and reactions; the second is more prose like and closer to the author's own speech. Prose descriptions would achieve much the same, but the laying out of the lines and the attention to imagery which poetry can promote, make these very evocative pieces.

Using free verse in PSHE

Writing in free verse enables children to write imaginatively, descriptively and with precision. And because free verse is often so very close to prose, every moment spent developing free verse writing will further enrich their prose.

Impossible Gifts

'Impossible gifts' is something I've adapted from a workshop by arguably our greatest guru in poetry writing with children, Fred Sedgwick, an activity that features in his book, 'Writing to Learn' (Routledge/Falmer). To open this workshop I read one of the 'Impossible gifts' poems written by children in one of my workshops, sometimes the ones on the following pages by Ryan or Cordelia.

I then ask the teacher, whilst I'm writing up a structure and ideas bank on the board, to ask the class: Why do we give gifts? When do we give gifts? Is it better to give or receive? What's the best present you have ever given? This gives me time to write the template/ideas list on the board, plus gets the class actively thinking about the whole concept. I'll explain that we are going to write a poem, a gift itself, to someone we admire. I write on the board:

For... Someone

These are the gifts
that I would
if I could
give to you...

I talk them through these opening lines, noting the alliteration in these/the/that, and the internal rhyme of would/could and the assonance of gifts/if/give and to/you.

From there, I'll take them through the ideas bank opposite, showing them potential sources for ideas, encouraging the class to really consider and explore these, and even mix and match some of these ideas to see what they come up with:

Impossible gifts - ideas

opposites: the **first**.../the **last**...

something **old** or **ancient**

something from the **future**

something from **space**

something from the **ocean**

something **extinct**

an aspect of an **animal** or **bird** (not just physical aspects, but qualities too, e.g. the stealth of a..., the patience of..., the wisdom of...)

something from **legends** or **mythology**

aspects of the four **seasons**

aspects of the five **senses**

something **invisible** or **silent**

I will write this next structure on the board:

> The ....
>   from/of a ....
> The ....
>   from/of a ....

and will take ideas from the class. If nothing happens initially, I might prompt them with questions like, 'What shining gift is at the bottom of the ocean?' or 'What gift is waiting out there in space?' These might lead to lines such as:

> The pearl
>   from a mermaid's purse
> The blazing trail
>   of a shooting star

I say to the class that although quantity isn't important, they should aim for at least eight lines. I ask the class to think of someone that they like/love/admire/miss, and to dedicate their poem to them. I say that the poem itself could become a gift. The title will be 'To...', then the name of the person that the poem is dedicated to. I make it clear that I want the reader, the recipient of the poem, to be moved by their words, their imagery, their generosity.

If children read out lines that are possible, I suggest ways of making them impossible, so 'the feather from a snowy owl' might become the 'the feather of a snow-white eagle'; 'a golden key' might become 'the lost key to the city of Atlantis'.

Here are two very different, but highly imaginative first draft versions of this poem.

To Grandad

If I could see you, these are the gifts
I would give to you if I could.

The spirit and melody of all the songs ever sung.

The gentle summer breeze on the Solstice.
The playfulness of a child wrapped in the most soft silk.
The dew on grass on crisp, autumnal mornings.
The simple sound of happiness catching the fresh, country air.

All the wonders of the Universe packed into a bag.

Grandad, when you look down on me, you give me as much advice as if you were sitting on my shoulder.
My tribute to you, being you.

All my love,
Ryan

**Ryan Walshaw, Year 6,
Rise Park Junior School**

To My Family

These are the gifts
for my family...

A blaze of fiery sunlight
the mist of a silvery ocean
or a smile from a wondrous dream
and the Seven Wonders of the World.

I would give to you
the life of a seamless wave
the breath of a restless lion
the dust of an elegant garment
the energy of a leaping stag
the first steps of a weary foal
the frantic leap of a hare
the icy silence of the whispering wind
the dancing shard of moonlight
across a still night
love for a newborn child

I would give to you...
the last sigh of the night.

Cordelia Dyter-Lyford, Year
7, St Paul's Catholic College

Beginnings: titles and opening lines of free verse poems

It is always good, where possible, to give children some kind of opening and idea of a title with free verse. Although the examples that follow are not linked to any particular school theme or topic, they could be adapted for use with many of the current Primary school topics.

An old favourite workshop of mine, this one – thankfully and frequently – gets some great results. I begin by putting this title and first line on the board:

Moonlit Midnight

Deep in the forest
there's ꓳ I ꓷ A M

I then ask the class to write a few non-rhyming lines to follow. Before I hear their ideas, I show the class some options of where they can go from there. I tell them that one boy said he thought of a wolf, and I put his idea up on the board:

A lonely wolf, padding through a snowy forest.

I tell the class that they could have this wolf in their own poems – or an arctic fox, or a snowy owl, or even an invented creature, say a snow-white eagle. So, what I am building up on the board is a smorgasbord of ideas, options where they can take their own version of the poem. More often than not I get a few clichés, like a 'hooting' owl and a 'howling' wolf. So I explain that the whole point of a poem is to say something fresh and so I might ask for other sounds that these creatures make and we might end up with:

I also demonstrate a call and response, along the lines of:

> Deep in the forest - there's ɔ I ɒ A M!
> Deep in the cave - there's mischief!
> Deep in the lake - there's mystery!
> Deep in the tree - there's madness

> Owls crying/chattering/weeping
> Wolves snarling/barking/whimpering

Boys frequently want to write about a 'scary' or 'spooky' forest, so then I explain that they need to 'show not tell'. 'Spooky' and 'scary' tell me nothing. I ask them to 'show' me 'spooky.' Are there eyes watching? Are their shadows following? Are there noises whirling all around?

I then go on to mention the five senses, for, as I explain, these bring your writing to life, make it deeper, more three-dimensional. I suggest that they could write a verse on each sense, in the list-style repetition structure:

Finally I ask them to give me some colourful verbs. I ask the class, 'What is the magic doing?' One child might say that it 'sparkles', so I'll set up four alliterating words:

> Deep in the forest
> there's ɔ I ɒ A M
> Magic that sparkles
> magic that spins
> magic that splutters
> magic that spreads...

> Deep in the forest
> there's ɔ I ɒ A M
> You can hear it
> echoing between the trees etc...
> You can see it
> leaping over rocks and stones   etc...
> You can feel it
> rumbling beneath your feet   etc...
> You can smell it
> rotting in the moss, the ferns   etc...

Moonlit Gathering

The moon hangs heavy over the hollow.
A bright full moon in a black night sky.
Out of the shadows, cats come stalking.
Into the hollow where the four oaks stand.
Spotted, tabby, black, white.
They gather there.
Twining tails, flashing eyes, rippling pelts
illuminated in the pale moon's glow.
Then onto a boulder four cats come leaping, yowling,
their bright eyes burning in the dark of the night.
The other cats look up, seeming to listen,
but there's nothing to hear.
Just twining tails, flashing eyes, rippling pelts
illuminated in the pale moon's glow.
Then the clouds roll in
and the moon is covered.
The bright silver hollow is dark once more.
As if by signal, the cats start leaving
and the hollow is empty, empty as before.
Silence, silence, but for the screeching of an owl,
and the whisper in the trees in the paler moon's glow.

Abigail Plant, Lake Middle School, IOW

This repetition-style alliteration can be done with all kinds of verbs, like glows/ glides/glitters/glimmers, dances/darts/ dips/dives and so on.

From there, I give the class carte blanche to write whatever they want about a forest. They do not have to use the starting point title/opening lines, but many do. Some change the title to one of their own, like 'Beneath the Magic Moon' or 'Midnight Forest'. Some do picture poems, even doing pieces in which the words form a path or stream through the forest.

That's a great poem above, isn't it? A first draft too. Clearly a young lady who adores reading and relishes language.

This way of writing, using a title and an opening line can be very effective. Using the same kind of brainstorming approach I have demonstrated above, here are other titles/openers:

The House On The Hill

Though empty
for many years

Moongazing

The moon
  looks different
    somehow

The Skaters

The lake is white
  the air is chilled
    the skaters...

Stormy Waters

The little boat
  was dragged by the tide
    out to where the waves raged

Conversation free verse poems

Children are good at dialogue. They read it in books and comics. They experience it in films and TV programmes and video games. So, the challenge is to find a creative framework for it, and to make it relevant and dynamic. What I did with 'Red & The Wolf' is to inject a little rhythm and rhyme into Wolf's speech to add to his menacing, bad guy address. So what this becomes is a hybrid of free verse/rhyming verse – but I would suggest that children stick to free verse where possible, as it will be simpler.

Perhaps the best known and most loved conversation poem is Harold Monro's delightful 'Overheard on a Saltmarsh', which is a real must for Upper KS2. Perfect for performance. Please Google it .

Conversation poems are like mini, concentrated dramas. Ideally, they take up no more than a page, and have simply two characters – as they are essentially duologues. The characters will only speak in short snippets, snappy phrases. If a conversation drifts, it will need to be pruned down. More than likely, a first draft will have far too much dialogue, too much detail. So, children will need to whittle their conversation poem down to a mini duologue that gets in, tells its story, and is done.

Warm ups – Write a conversation poem between:

- Goldilocks and Baby Bear

- Rapunzel and the Prince

- The Tortoise and the Hare

- The Troll and the Billy Goats Gruff

- Cinderella and her sisters

Possible scenarios:

- **Victorians** – Victorian teacher and pupil, or employer and child labourer

- **Ancient Egyptians** – pyramid builder and slave

Red & The Wolf

And who are you, The Hood in the Wood?

Not saying.

I bet you're a chatterbox. Yap. Yap. Yap.

Not saying.

It's not much fun when the cat's got your tongue!

Still not saying.

Is that food, Little Hood? Smells good!

Not saying anything.

To Granny's perhaps, with your yummy snacks?

Not speaking to a beast like you.

Here's a cunning plan – take the short cut to your Gran's!

How did you know that?

With great big ears you can really hear.

You were listening to me and my mum, weren't you?

Right, Red Hood, I'll beat you good.
As quick as a hare, I'll race you there!

James Carter

- **Tudors** – Henry VIII and one of his subjects or wives

- **Romans** – a Roman soldier and a Celt

Conversation poems are also ideal for classes studying a particular story or novel, as they can hone in on one moment from a story, and expand and explore it in a dramatic conversation, for example, a Tracy Beaker conversation with her adopted mother, Cam – or a Harry Potter conversation between Harry and the house-elf Dobby. Once you have chosen your novel/characters, you might wish to do a quick character brainstorm first, and think of adjectives to describe the two characters, and how they react in certain situations.

Shape poems and calligrams

It hardly needs to be said that children really enjoy doing shape poetry. But teachers are often frustrated with the results, as children can focus more on the shape rather than the words. The answer is simple: start by writing a poem, say a rhyming poem or a kenning. Work on these until they are ready, drafted, finished and then the poems can be put into shapes in three ways:

- Draw the outline of the subject and put the words inside. Animal kennings are great for shapes. You write and finish the poem first. Then you cut out the animal shape on card, and put the words inside. These make great mobiles.

Tree

A tree
is not like you and
me – it waits around quite
patiently – catching kites and
dropping leaves – reaching out to touch
the breeze…A tree all day will stand and stare
clothed in summer, winter: bare – it has no shame
or modesty…Perhaps its generosity is the greatest in
the world – it gives a home to every bird, every squirrel,
feeds them too – to every dog it is a loo…And after dark
what does it do? Catch a falling star or two? Shimmy
in the old moonlight? Or maybe have a conker fight?
A tree can give an awful lot: the wood to make a
baby's cot – pencils, paper, tables, chairs – lolly
sticks as well as stairs …Without a tree we
could not live – a tree, it seems just
loves to give –
but us:
we
chop
we
take
we
burn
that's
what we
do in return

James Carter
(Time-travelling
Underpants, Macmillan
Children's Books)

What To Say If You Meet A Ghost...

```
            Aaa
          aaaaaaa
          aaaaaaa
!!!       aaaaaa        !!!
!!        aaaaa          !!
   !!      aaa        !!
   !!    aaaaaaa    !!
     aaaaaaaaaaaaaa
    aaaaaaaaaaaaaaaa
   aaaaaaaaaaaaaaaaaaa
  aaaaaaaaaaaaaaaaaaaa
   aaaaaaaaaaaaaaaaaa
    aaaaaaaaaaaaaaaa
      aaaaaaaaaaaa
       aaaaaaaaaa
        aaaaaaa
          hhhh
           hhh
           hhh
            hh
            hh
             h
             !
          !
      !

!
```

James Carter

Little
Alien!

```
      ???    ???
       ??  ??
       ??  ??
       ??  ??
       I'm a
     little alien,
    can't you see,
    the grooviest
        guy
         in
        the
    galaxy? I'm
   !! curious, and that !!
   !!  is why – around the   !!
 !!   universe I fly: and whizz  !!
 !!   about the rings of Saturn,   !!
 !!   Milky Way's great swirly   !!
  !!   pattern, and Mars, the  !!
   !!   stars, the moon, the  !!
   !!   sun ... I'm a little   !!
      alien. Life is
          fun!
        !!    !!
       !!      !!
       !!       !!
       !!       !!
        !!     !!
       !!!!!   !!!!!
```

James Carter

- Make the words form the shape of the subject. This is harder, although I've seen some great shape poems done this way by Year 5 and 6 classes.

- Type your poem, slowly and word by word into a PC. Put the cursor in the middle of the page. Even type a word or two per line. Experiment with different line lengths. Say you wanted to do something with 'Oh tiny star, how white, how bright…', you could try typing it out as:

> oh
> tiny
> star how
> white how bright…

and a star pattern slowly emerges.

Have a look at the ghost and the alien shape poems opposite. See how they use punctuation to form part of the image – exclamation and question marks. You could also try including these, as well as commas, ampersands, etc.

Calligram poems (see 'Saturn' p39) are also popular, and lots of fun for all Primary Key Stages. Calligrams are words that are made to look like what they mean, such as:

wobbly spotty
LARGE

and are most frequently done with firework poems every November. But calligrams can be used to spice up all kinds of writing, including poetry, and children can have real fun playing with fonts, sizes, shadowing effects using word processing programs or apps.

Riddles make great calligram-style poems:

Who Was I?

Your
GREATEST
King.
I was **TALL** but **round.**
CREATIVE
yet **PROUD**
and AGGRESSIVE.
FEaRED by my *many* **wives**...

Try a Queen Victoria calligram poem (or another ruler/icon or celebrity), or even one based on a nation – the Aztecs, Celts, Saxons, Vikings or Ancient Egyptians.

Acrostics and alphabets

I'm ambivalent about acrostics. On the one hand children are attracted to the simple structure that they provide but, long-term, acrostics can provide an unwanted default mode or a safety net in which children no longer take risks with their writing. One year a library held a poetry competition. 75% of the entries were acrostics. The best poems were, predictably, the other 25%. Acrostics force children to use letters that might not give anything to a topic, and the same applies to rhyme. A far better, though less-used acrostic form is the mid-line acrostic, also known as a 'mesostic'. Much easier to do, it results in there being no random words or phrases injected because it allows children to use words and phrases that they actually want to use.

This mid-line acrostic is actually an extended sentence, and simply highlights the key word VIKINGS:

TheSe braVe warriorS
travelled from ScandInavia
to Kingdoms acroSS Europe
as far as Iceland, and
America, tradiNg,
stealinG, settling
telling theirSagas wherever they went.

And this dragon one deliberately plays with alliteration to add music to the poem, as well as each line serving as a simile:

Wings as wiDe as ancient oceans
eyes of molten crystal ambeR
teeth as shArp as a white shark's fin
tail of a miGhty python
scales of gOrgeous golden green
jaws that ever huNger
breath stolen from the Sun

This minibeasts mid-line acrostic is simply a list of bugs.

WorMs
LadybIrds
ANts
SnaIls
bed Bugs
CatErpillars
wASps
MoSquitoes
BeeTles
GraSShoppers

I've started this autumn (a hardy perennial topic, ho ho!) mid-line acrostic – please finish off…

It's September Again
and autumn says goodbye to sUmmer

A double alphabet with transport/places:

Let's go by...

Aeroplane to Africa
Bus to Butlins
Car to Canada
Diesel train to Disneyland
Eurostar to Europe
Ferry to Florida
Gondola to Greece
Helicopter to Hungerford
Inter-city to India
Jeep to Japan
Kawasaki to Kintbury
Lorry to London
Motorbike to Madagascar
Narrowboat to Newbury
Oxen to Oxford
Pony & trap to Paris
Quad bike to Quebec
Rail to Reading
Scooter to Swindon
Tractor to Turkey
Underground to Uganda
Van to Venezuela
Waggon to West Wales
X-reg Volvo to eXeter
Yak to York
Zebra to Zanzibar

Year 1 and 2 classes with James Carter, Kintbury St Mary's CE Primary School, West Berkshire

Another version of this alphabet acrostic could feature food and places:

Let's Eat...

Avocados in Africa
Buns in Brazil
Carrots in Canada

Animal alphabets are always popular.

I went on
  An animal hunt
    And I saw...

Awesome armadillos
Boisterous bears
Crafty crocodiles
Daft ducks
Elegant elephants...

There are exceptions to every rule – for, if done properly with thought, craft and creativity, an opening line acrostic can work extremely well, as with this rainforest acrostic below, which was written as part of a class topic. The language is vivid and image-rich, those five senses really come to the fore, and Lily follows the poets' maxim of 'show don't tell':

Rhythmic clicking echoes of crickets passing by

Amazing Amazonian hibiscus flowers peeking out from the forest floor

Inspirational wonders all around

Natural habitats to fascinating and tropical plants

Frogs with bulging eyes flash red when caught by surprise

Occasional silent moments amongst the bursts of loud noise

Rustling leaves of snakes passing through

Exotic birds fill the air with chirping songs

Shimmering waterfalls appear to drop from the sky

The vegetation lays dark, damp and humid like a steamy sauna

Lily Phillips, Falkland Primary School

Other ways to stimulate ideas for poetry writing

So, poetry writing needs to originate from many sources, not just as writing for the sake of writing. What's essential is that it's not all about structures, models and 'scaffolds'. That, as useful an approach as it is, can be too rigid, formulaic and prescriptive a methodology that, if used in isolation, will inevitably and often result in bland, lifeless fill-in-the-gaps writing.

Moreover, many teachers concur that 'literacy' (that dreaded lacklustre word again!) has become too much of 'here are the rules, apply them yourself'. So, what to do? I think the answer is to not consciously think 'what is the poetic structure/rule here?' or 'what poetic framework can I apply?' but to let words evolve organically, and to let the subject matter and context decide where the words want to go, what shape or form the piece wants to take. What could be better than grabbing a piece of large-scale sugar paper, getting down on the carpet with the class and throwing a bunch of words, phrases and ideas down and see where they want to go and what they want to be. What sounds do they make? Shall we write some words big, some small, some even sdrawkcab?

As a writer-in-schools I have to remind myself that words shouldn't always be the starting point for more words. Children need to regularly experience things emotionally, viscerally, intellectually, spiritually, long before the issue of writing should be brought up.

My personal favourite medium for generating thoughts and writing is music, as it gives a freedom to write like nothing else – it lets children get lost in what I call 'the fog of their creativity', and lost in the magical process of dreaming and of writing. It does not matter if the end product is not always great, it's the immersion and enjoyment of the process that matters most. How easy is it to put some music on (ideally some atmospheric instrumental music) once a week and let them write literally whatever they want for fifteen minutes?

Here are a few diverse ways into stimulating ideas for writing:

Discussions

Have PSHE or circle-time discussions on a whole range of topics and issues, for example:

O My hopes and ambitions

O A lonely moment

O What makes me mad

O Jealousy

O The time I surprised myself

O If I could change one thing about school

Why not even try some zany and unusual discussions:

O I'm going to invent a brand new colour – it's…

O At the bottom of the sea is a…

O What would aliens think of us humans?

O A secret I've kept until now

O If I was the boss of the universe I'd…

- Better than a jar of sweets is a jar of…

- I'd like to invent a…

- If pigs could fly, then…

Go for it! For all of these topics, free verse poems would often be the most suitable medium.

Photos, cuttings from magazines, postcards, Google Images

Hurrah for Google Images! Instant access to infinite galleries of fabulous images. What's more, children so readily take to using pictures, paintings, photographs and images as stimuli for writing. One very creative way of doing this is to not just use one single picture, but put various photographs, illustrations, even postcards together to see if some narrative or story or idea occurs. From there, children can brainstorm ideas and simply take their pencils for a walk and see what writing emerges. And, as with music there is no singular or 'correct' response. Within reason, any creative response is valid. Whatever an image sparks off, that's fine, follow it to see where it might go.

The highly influential Aidan Chambers' approach to using various stimuli (including books) is to ask simple, open-ended questions. So, first go to Google Images and source an image, perhaps a painting. You could try something like 'Gypsy with Lion' or 'Surprised!' by Henri Rousseau, or 'Sleep' by Salvador Dali or 'Three Musicians' by Picasso. With the image on your interactive board, say to the class 'Tell me about this.' Or 'What's happening here?' Or 'What would the painting say if it could speak?' 'What music would you put to this painting?' Or (if relevant) 'Write down the thoughts of the character in the picture.' Or 'Write a conversation between two people in the picture.'

If you want to move into a writing stage, you could ask, 'If this was a poem/story, what would it say?'

Music

Increasingly KS2 classes have music playing during extended writing sessions. This is great, as music certainly helps to focus the creative mind, and allow the mind to go off to other places and find unusual, unexpected and innovative ideas. Equally exciting is to use the music as a stimulus itself. Play music that children respond to creatively. Instrumental music, such as classical or film soundtracks are often best. (Songs with lyrics are too language-specific for this use.)

Scour YouTube, Spotify or iTunes for suitable pieces, anything instrumental with atmosphere will do. Try movie soundtracks, World music, classical music, but something the children will not recognise and have automatic associations with. (Brian Eno's instrumental music is also ideal. Try his Apollo soundtrack.) Play the music a few times, and ask the children to gather words, phrases, images, perhaps a narrative or story thread. Why not play quiet music during carpet time and ask the children to come up with language and ideas that the music suggests. My book 'Just Imagine' (Taylor & Francis) contains a CD of original music for this very purpose.

Real experiences/ School trips

Farms, zoos, museums, National Trust homes, beaches, residential trips etc. – visits to all kinds of places give children real experiences to then use as starting points for poems. And there is no reason why children can't make notes – words, phrases, images whilst on the visit itself. Good forms for such experiences are 'Free Verse' p92 and 'Syllabic Poetry' p90.

Drama

Drama enables children to engage in so many issues, as well as stories, emotions, feelings. It also develops confidence and performance/public-speaking skills. Working in pairs can naturally lead to conversation poems (see p105). Here are some opening lines:

○ Why didn't you invite me to…?

○ Why are you acting so strangely?

○ What's that thing I saw in your bag?

○ Look, I've got a great idea…

○ Look what I invented…

For group work, you could try scenarios such as:

○ Getting to know a new child in a class.

○ Someone gets in trouble for something they didn't do.

○ Someone has to own up to… and so on. As a result, children can write short prose pieces or free verse poems in the voice of their character.

Artefacts

Artefacts are wonderful for opening up possibilities and ideas which can later lead to some form of writing. Ideally, you will take in something old – say a painting, a hat, a gas mask or a musical instrument. The simple openers 'Who? What? Why? Where? When?' will stimulate some useful ideas. Children can even volunteer to hot seat: 'This is the hat worn by an evacuee child during World War II' or 'This instrument has magical powers. Whoever plays it goes into a trance and…' A trip to a charity shop or car boot sale might lead you to some inexpensive artefacts too.

Section Four - Developing children as poets

Let's Respond to Poetry

Responding to children's writing

Perhaps the most important, but most obvious point to make is that when reading a child's poem, we need to solely focus on the composition. A piece of creative writing is not the place to discuss handwriting, punctuation, grammar, spelling etc. This will only serve to confuse and demotivate a child, and perhaps quash their creativity. Clearly, emphasising the positive aspects of their writing is essential, but you will also need to be warmly critical as well. The tried and tested method is to begin with a compliment and then to hone in on something that needs work. Say, 'Sophie – you have a great title there, and the opening works really well, but that second line needs a little bit of a tweak, perhaps you could try another adjective here…' and so on.

Publishing is a great motivator, and I've noticed that children are even encouraged by having a word or phrase of theirs put on the board as I am scribing a poem. Sometimes children have a great idea that won't work in a specific context, so why not try suggesting 'That's a lovely idea, why not write about that in a poem later?'

or Stephen Bowkett's fabulous phrase [sic] 'Keep that as a little treasure in your pocket for later on.' If children know that their poems will be published on a class display, in a class book, on the school website or in a school anthology (see LET'S LIVE POETRY: Publishing p16) or even read out in an assembly or concert, they will be happy (hopefully) to put that extra bit of time and effort into it.

As I've said before in this book, try and avoid the word 'draft'. It sounds too onerous and dull. Try 'tweak' or 'crafting'. Sounds better already, doesn't it? Showing children copies of poems that have been drafted by professional poets (see my poem and draft of 'How To Build A Dragon' on the following page) always helps to demonstrate that a poem never comes together in one sitting, but can often take days, weeks, months to refine and craft. And children also need to be aware that each poem will have its own individual process, journey, number of tweaks. Some can come together reasonably quickly, others may take arduous drafting, but the reader will never know from the final result.

Perhaps the simplest acid test for a poem is to read it aloud to the child, and then they can more objectively hear the poem's strengths and weaknesses, and from there you can discuss what needs to be done next.

The checklist on the next page provides you with ideas as to how to improve and develop a child's poem. Each poem is unique, and there is no set template to follow, though these areas will help the young writer and you to consider the growing poem from a variety of angles to see how it is coming along, and what further work may need to be done.

Further to the checklist is a brief section 'How can I grow as a poet?' which contains specific advice to young poets on various aspects of writing. You may wish to read some of this out to the class or create a poster with 'top tips'.

Please show your class the two drafts of 'How To Build A Dragon' below. Ask them to compare the first/second draft and the final draft (as much as they can). Which is better, and why? Where possible, compare words, lines and phrases from each.

How To Build A Dragon

Take…

The **cunning** of a trickster
the **cruelty** of a storm
the **loneliness** of mountains
the **shock** of early dawn

The **hunger** of the winter
the **shiver** of a tomb
the **madness** and the
strangeness
of the **dark** side of the **moon**

The **blazing** of the mighty sun
the **anger** of a king
the **elegance** and **deadly dance**
of **eagles** on the wing

Now find a **cave** to work in
a **cauldron** deep and strong
with **care**, mix these ingredients
and toil from **dusk** to **dawn**

And when you see that **dragon** rise
be **quick** – be out – just run
though you have made a **life** anew
yours may soon be **done**…

James Carter

Poetry checklist - what to look out for when writing a new poem

Structure

Title – A title is more important than people think, for it is the doorway into the poem. Generally speaking, you want to entice or intrigue the reader with your title, without going over the top. Sometimes something as simple as 'The Night' will do.

Opening – Does the poem begin well? Does it grab the reader's attention? Does it feel right? As an experiment, what would happen if you began with, say the third line or the second verse?

Middle – Does the poem develop well? Does it say what you want it to say? Do you keep to the feel, the rhythm, the mood, the voice?

End – Do you have the right ending? If in doubt, think of a few alternatives and find the one that works best.

Sequence – Try reading the lines/verses in a different order. Could you move them around to create a better order and flow?

Language – general

- Do the words say what you want them to?
- Could you use fewer words or do you need more to give depth and detail?

- Is your language original? Do you have any clichés?
- Are you using strong, expressive verbs and adjectives?
- Could you use some of the five senses to bring the writing to life even more?

Rhyme

- Does your poem rhyme? If so, would it work better if it didn't?
- Are you using random/lazy rhymes that make no sense in the poem?
- If a rhyme doesn't work well, could you think of a different word or even rephrase the line?

Rhythm

- How does the poem feel? Read it out loud.
- How does it sound?
- Does it flow well? Is it bumpy or awkward in places?
- If a rhyming poem, count the syllables in each line. Do you have roughly the same number in each line?
- Could you add or cut words?
- Ask someone to read it out loud to you – that's always the best test!

Poetry checklist - what to look out for when writing a new poem (continued)

Originality: similes and metaphors

The poet Robert Frost said that 'Poetry is a fresh look and a fresh listen', which means trying to avoid any clichés. Try to avoid stale phrases such as 'the owl hoots'; instead, try 'the owl chatters' or 'the owl cries'.

Are you using old similes such as 'hissed like a snake' or metaphors like 'it was raining cats and dogs'? These are fine for a first draft, but in a second or third draft could be changed and improved upon. Again, it's not about using difficult or long words, it's about finding simple but new ways of saying, seeing and describing things.

Effect

- Does the poem bring out the mood or the message that you want it to?

- If it's a funny poem will it make the reader laugh? Can you try it out on someone?

- If the poem is a thoughtful poem, will it make your readers think about your subject?

Imagery

Do you show rather than tell? Rather than 'it was a spooky house' could you try 'the house of shadows whispered to itself at night', or instead of 'the moon was beautiful' could you be more expressive and visual and 'show' by saying, 'the single silver eye of the moon reflected deep within the glassy lake'.

Be a reader and a writer

Imagine you had not written your poem yourself – what would you think of the poem then? Think: are you, the writer, entertaining you the reader? What do you like to read? What writing excites you? What could you borrow and make your own? And don't worry, all writers are influenced by others, borrow ideas from others, and that's fine, so long as you change it significantly to make it your own.

Let it go

Not every poem will be as good as you want it to be, or even get finished off. This is natural. Poets often discard poems that aren't working, but keep certain phrases or lines for when they are working on new poems.

How can I grow as a poet? Ways in which young poets can develop their writing

Read and **read** and **read**... and keep reading. And read everything, from novels to plays, non-fiction to poetry. Good writers are good readers.

Read as a writer – As you read, look out for words, phrases, tricks, devices, structures you could adopt and adapt for your own writing. But do 'make it your own' – for, if you do take something, you have to change it enough so that it becomes something fresh, new and different. And don't worry, all writers – from Shakespeare to J. K. Rowling – have borrowed things. The trick is to borrow from all over, read as widely as you can, and then create a style of your own.

Show don't tell – Beware of bland adjectives! 'The beautiful night' and 'the spooky forest' tell us nothing. 'The sky was awash with crystal stars' and 'the shadows of the forest wriggled in the breeze' demonstrate a great deal, and in very few words.

Less is more – A poem has so few words, so every single syllable has to count. Don't be afraid to cut, cut, cut when you edit. Beware of too many adjectives and adverbs. Which of these is better: 'he walked slowly...' or 'he staggered...'? More than anything else, the poet's motto is 'The right word in the right place.'

Five senses – These make writing come to life. A flat piece of writing can come alive and become three-dimensional by simply adding sounds, smells, textures and so on.

First thoughts – The first thing you think of for a poem won't necessarily be the opening. It might be the middle or the end, or just a stepping stone to get you into the poem. (Sometimes you lose the original seed of an idea, as it is not needed in the poem.)

Take time – Don't expect too much of a first or second draft. The best editor of a poem is time. Leave your poem for at least a few days and then come back to it and read it not as a writer, but as a reader, and see what has to be done next. Ask others to read it, and give you feedback. Ask others to read it aloud to you. How does it sound?

Be adventurous – It's not what you say, but how you say it. And it's not about using long or complicated words, but using adventurous new ways of describing things that can bring any type of writing to life. It can just be a simple adjective or verb, or an unusual simile or metaphor. A first draft will bring automatic writing like 'the dark night was as cold as ice' but with time and work, it can become 'the night was winter-cold, dark as a tomb'.

Bring out as much as you can...in a first sitting. And when you find a good idea, try and get out as many ideas, words, thoughts, phrases, lines, verses as you can. All of this may prove vital later. This way, you have got a lot of material to use when you work on it further.

Let's Take it Further

Organising a visit from a poet

Why invite a poet in? Where do I start? Okay…you're getting an expert in, someone who writes and reads and performs and workshops for a living. Having a poet in is a lot of fun. It's a whole day dedicated to the joy of language. The children get so much out of it, and so do the teachers. It's a kind of INSET day – watching how poetry can be brought to life.

Long gone are the days when a poet could stand at the front of the hall, shuffle a few manuscript pages around and open up with 'Good morning, children. I'm going to read you some new poems. Who can tell me what a poem is?' For a start, children – particularly KS2 – expect to be entertained. So, the new breed of children's poets use instruments – guitars, drums, percussion, ukuleles and so forth – as well as props and costumes. Some do magic tricks and juggle. Poets do many things to keep those children entertained. They move around the hall. They invite children up to read, to chant, to get involved, to participate. Some do stand-up comedy between poems. They get children to clap along, impersonate things, join in during the choruses.

I estimate that there are some several hundred of us 'real live poets' (as teachers insist on calling us!) regularly walking the boards of Primary schools. Some of these poets are high-profile names, some not so well-known, some not even published at all – but are simply great with words and at getting children switched on to writing. Whatever the status of each poet, children need to see that poems are written by everyday people who simply have a talent for using and crafting language, and a love of sharing it with others, for demythologising the writing process, and for encouraging others into the word thing.

If I'm to be honest, the success of a day depends very much upon the teachers. Children are always fantastic – they're usually responsive and keen to enjoy some musical language. But it's how the teachers approach and frame the day and 'big up' that experience for the children that really counts. On those days where the children have done research on my poetry featured on my website, prepared some questions, maybe even worked up a performance of one of my poems for me, the experience couldn't be better. Everyone gets so much out of the day. Only very occasionally – maybe once every five years (if that) – I'll feel that I'm simply there to tick a box so that they can tell OFSTED they've had a poet in. On those days, the teachers do their marking as you are performing and workshopping, and even chat amongst themselves (or worse still, leave the room) – but I'm too cheeky a visitor to let that happen for any length of time!

Beyond 100% teacher involvement, the success of a day with a poet is all down to one thing: good organisation. So where to begin? Perhaps a teacher or group of teachers have identified the need for a poet, to come into the school, to motivate and inspire both children and adults alike.

How to get hold of a poet

Most teachers tell me that they Google 'children's poets' and start from there. You will ideally need to do this a term or two before the event. I'm sure you will come across website addresses of many poets active in Primary schools. You might come up with a few agencies such as Speaking of Books, Class Act, Agency, Authors Abroad and Book A Poet. Agencies cost a little more, but do a lot of the groundwork for you, and help you to find the right person. Why not ring up other local schools to see if they can recommend anyone?

Who to choose

'I want William Shakespeare. He must visit us on National Poetry Day, and visit Reception, KS1 and KS2. And I want him to write minibeast sonnets with Year 1 and…'

Hang on there! Perhaps Will won't be available. Personally, I would keep an open mind at this stage. The bigger the name, the more they will cost, the less likely they are to do writing workshops, and the more likely they will be booked up a long way in advance.

How to organise a day

Having visited 1000+ schools, the timetable I have ended up with works well in most Primaries and for most poets:

- KS2 assembly in hall (30 minutes)

- KS1 assembly in hall (30 minutes)

- Visit to Reception (15 minutes)

- Four or so workshops, usually at KS2 (in classrooms, 40 minutes each approx.)

- Finale in hall – children reading poems from workshops

- Bookselling/signing

In a two-form entry school, we double up the classes, squeeze the children into one class for 15 minutes while we brainstorm a poem, then split the classes up to get writing.

If it's a Junior school, there's this adapted version:

- Years 3 and 4 assembly in hall (30 minutes)

- Years 5 and 6 assembly in hall (30 minutes)

- Four or so workshops (in classrooms, 40 minutes each approx.)

- Finale in hall – children reading poems from workshops

- Bookselling/signing

- Or, if the hall will allow, bring all years in together for an assembly at the end of the day.

If it's an Infant school, there's this adapted version:

- KS1 assembly in hall (30 minutes)

- Visit to Reception (15 minutes)

- Visit to Nursery (15 minutes)

- Four or so workshops at KS1 (in classrooms, 40 minutes each approx.)

- Finale in hall – children reading poems from workshops

- Book selling/signing

But each poet will do something slightly different. As I've said, the very big names often don't do workshops at all, and will more likely offer something like three 1-hour performances or talks. So, it's up to the teacher organising the event if they want the big name, or a lesser-known individual who is happy to offer both performances and workshops.

what to ask

- Whether emailing an agency or poet direct, give them a choice of dates. Try and be flexible.

- Ask how much experience the poet has of visiting schools.

- Ask for a reference and a CRB.

- Ask for samples of their work if you need to.

- Ask if they do Foundation, KS1 and KS2. Most do.

- Ask what type of material they will do in performance and in workshops.

- Personally, I would ask if they do a

range of both serious and funny poems. Non-stop funnies does nobody any favours, and the job description is 'poet' not 'comedian'. One KS1 teacher in Inverness rightly told me 'When poets just do funnies, the children start laughing and stop listening.'

- Some teachers ask if poets do workshops that might tie in with each class's topics. This can work both ways. Sometimes it is better to let a poet come in and do their tried and tested workshops. Alternatively, you might have chosen for a poet to come in and help the school/classes explore and celebrate all kinds of things, from Science or Japan/Brazil/Africa week, or shape poems or the natural world. It won't do any harm asking the poet, but bear in mind, you may well be asking them to do a workshop they have never tried out before. However, they may have a model or form (say raps, haikus, kennings) that can be adapted to that theme/topic.

- Ask what the poet wants to achieve from the day.

- Ask, if relevant to your needs, if they do INSET or Gifted and talented writers' days.

Organising a Poet-In-Residence

These are wholly different experiences to a single day. A good residency, one that is well organised and well thought through, will have **numerous long-term benefits**.

Some residencies last only a few days, but to make a real impact, I would argue that you need five or six days, and ideally these would be spread over a few weeks, to maximise the impact. These residences will benefit staff, children and even the community. During five days or so, there will be time for all kinds of wonderful activities.

A Case Study of a residency

Below is an overview of a recent residency I undertook at the fabulous Kintbury St Mary's CE Primary School in West Berkshire, a one-form entry school, with one class per year group.

The residency was funded by the very hardworking PTA, and the residency was set up by Class Act Agency. This is how the five days panned out:

I had a number of telephone conversations with the Headteacher some weeks before the residency began,

Day one – Separate performances for KS2, KS1 and Reception. Then poetry writing workshops with Years 3, 4, 5 and 6. To finish the day, a one-hour 'twilight INSET'. Although twilights are not ideal, this was more to get to know the teachers, to show them a few poetry games and to get them writing with me.

Day two – Further poetry workshops around the classrooms: revisits to Years 3, 4, 5 and 6 and first workshops with Years 1 and 2.

Day three – Return to Reception class for more action rhymes and riddles. Writing workshops in all KS2 and KS1 classes. To finish the day, an after-school family-writing session. This was very well attended. We did fairytale raps, and much fun was had.

Day four – Poetry performance workshops in all the classrooms from Reception to Year 6.

Day five – Workshops in the hall all day. Individual children practising their poems to read and whole classes running through their performance pieces. To finish the residency, a Poetry Finale with parents in attendance at the end of the day, each class doing a number of poems and performances.

Evening event (one term later) – A gala of poetry, songs, music, dancing, and all kinds, from the children – to celebrate the publication of the Kintbury St Mary's poetry anthology (printed by www.thelittlebooks.co.uk), which features poems written throughout the residency.

discussing dates, numbers of workshops per day, and what we wanted to achieve overall. Originally, the residency was to take place in one week, but I persuaded the school that the impact would be greater if spread over two weeks. The Headteacher wanted me to come in and spend equal time across the Key Stages. I offered her both writing and performance workshops, twilight INSET and an after-school family session and a finale to finish, on the last day – all of which she was very happy with. She asked if I would tie in with the class topics where possible, which I did at both KS1 and KS2. (Some residencies I have done since have also included a Years 5 and 6 and Years 3 and 4 G&T strand.)

This was a most rewarding and successful residency for a number of reasons – the high level of interest and commitment from the teachers, the support of the Headteacher throughout, the hard work of the PTA, the warm encouragement from the parents, and of course, the enthusiasm and positivity from all the children!

A few months on, I did a second 5-day residency, this one set up by myself and the literacy co-ordinator, in a two-form entry school – the wonderful Falklands Primary School in nearby Newbury. We followed a very similar model to the one at Kintbury St Mary's, but I simply doubled up the workshops each day, working with two classes at a time.

A Poetry Week

This could be an alternative to the ever-prevalent book week, and hey, why not have one at an unusual time (i.e. not to coincide with National Poetry Day – the first Thursday in October or World Book Day – the first Thursday in March), say mid-November,

before the mad pre-Christmas rush, in early January to shake off the New Year blues or late May/early June to celebrate no more assessments! Here are just a few ideas:

Invite a poet in! see p120.

Teachers visit each other's classes to read their favourite poem(s).

Have a poetry reading in the staffroom – During one lunch break, have teachers reading poems they have written/their favourites. This can be a real hoot, and a great bonding exercise for staff.

Put on a poetry show – Each class performs a poem, teachers/headteacher/parents/governors read too.

Visit the poetry society website – It has plenty of useful resources for teachers – www.poetrysociety.org.uk.

Publish a book of poems written during the week – illustrated/designed by the children. Perhaps you know of a local printing company that would do this at a reasonable rate – include some local advertising, and that might pay for some/all of it. Or even try www.thelittlebooks.co.uk

Dress up as characters from poems and nursery rhymes and rhyming picture books (e.g. the Gruffalo).

Redecorate doors as covers to poetry books – 'Revolting Rhymes', 'The Jolly Postman', 'Don't Put Mustard in the Custard', 'Please Mrs Butler', 'The Gruffalo' etc. or, have characters from nursery rhymes or rhyming picture books.

Put a giant poem on your door! Choose some neat writers to copy out a chosen poem (not too long – one with just a few verses would do) onto a door-sized sheet of paper. Other children can decorate.

Write a school rap – There must be a teacher/TA who would volunteer to do this, maybe in conjunction with children from KS2. It could be done in a lunchtime or two. Perhaps the rap could be about the history of the school, recent events/achievements, funny moments and so on.

Print out copies of poems – Plaster them everywhere: in the hall, the loos, displays, corridors, in the newsletter, everywhere! Poems by children, teachers, published poems, all kinds.

Have a book fair – The unrivalled Travelling Book Company always carry a good supply of poetry books, amongst other titles – fiction and non-fiction, but if you ask them as you make arrangements, they will include an extra supply of great poetry titles – www.travellingbooks.co.uk

Try a poetry trail – Devised by poet megastar Brian Moses, and in his own words… 'A Writers' Trail can be established around the school grounds, the school's immediate neighbourhood, an ancient building, a park, or along a stretch of seafront. Ideally the trail should have 10 or 12 stopping points where children can be stimulated to write in a variety of genres. Each point on the trail should then have a range of activities to suit children of different ages and abilities. Some of the ideas will spring from discussion with the children themselves and initially a small group of older children could act as trail coordinators. Points on a trail can be given interesting names rather than just point 1 or point 2, e.g. Lily Pad Pond, Crusoe's cabin (a gardener's hut), Dragon ash (site of a bonfire), the 'Y' tree (from the shape of its branches).' Try Brian's blog and website – www.brianmoses.co.uk

Try a poetry installation – The poetry 'tree' with poems on leaves/branches has always been popular in Primary schools, but why not go further? Have a poetry 'installation', i.e. an area (and yes, this can involve a tree too) in a public space in the school – say the school hall or library or reception. Why not decorate the area with poetry books, photocopied poems, anthologies that the classes have made? Have an 'add a line' poem – the teacher/class write the first verse then visitors to the installation come and add a new line each. Photocopy poems written by one class that other classes can illustrate. Also, children at set times could perform live in the installation, in character or reading and acting out pieces. Have video/sound recordings playing too. What's not to like?

Let's Recommend

Poems and poets

A single poetry book is not going to give you everything you need. It's best to have a handful – or hey, several shelves full – of anthologies as well as some single author collections.

Single poet collections are good for getting to know a particular poet well, finding out what voice(s) they write in, what themes they address, seeing how they deal with a range of tones and forms. Poetry anthologies give a wider experience overall as they offer readers a range of poets, often on a single theme or a number of related themes.

Nowadays we tend to gravitate towards the recent and the modern, yet classic poets are always worth a look at, and give a very different reading experience to children. Try Robert Louis Stevenson, Ted Hughes, Walter de la Mare, Edward Lear, A. A. Milne, Lewis Carroll, and of course, Charles Causley.

Single poet collections

Allan Ahlberg – Please Mrs Butler/Heard it in the Playground/Collected Poems/Friendly Matches (Puffin)

Roald Dahl – Revolting Rhymes/Dirty Beasts (Puffin)

Carol Ann Duffy – New and Collected Poems for Children (Faber & Faber)

Roger McGough – Bad, Bad Cats/You Tell me (with Michael Rosen)/All The Best (all Puffin)

Tony Mitton – Plum/Come Into This Poem (Francis Lincoln)/Big Bad Raps series (Orchard)

Brian Patten – Thawing Frozen Frogs, Juggling with Gerbils (Puffin)

Michael Rosen – Centrally Heated Knickers (Puffin)/Mustard, Custard, Grumble Belly and Gravy (Bloomsbury)

Kit Wright – The Magic Box (Macmillan)

Benjamin Zephaniah – Talking Turkeys/Funky Chickens (Puffin)

Poetry anthologies

Pumpkin Grumpkin – nonsense poems/A Caribbean Dozen – John Agard & Grace Nichols (Walker Books)

Orange Silver Sausage – poems without rhymes – ed. James Carter & Graham Denton (Walker Books)

The Works – ed. Paul Cookson, Pie Corbett, Brian Moses et al (Macmillan)

A First Poetry Book – chosen by Pie Corbett and Gaby Morgan (Macmillan Children's Books)

The Puffin Book of Fantastic First Poems – ed. June Crebbin (Puffin)

My Cat is in Love with the Goldfish/When Granny Won Olympic Gold – Graham Denton (Bloomsbury)

This Little Puffin (Puffin)

Sensational! Poems inspired by the five senses – ed. Roger McGough (Macmillan)

The Ring of Words – ed. Roger McGough (Faber)

A First Poetry Book – Gaby Morgan & Pie Corbett (Macmillan)

The Puffin Book of Utterly Brilliant Poetry/ The Puffin Book of 20th Century Children's Verse – both ed. by Brian Patten (Puffin)

Michael Rosen's A–Z – Michael Rosen (Puffin)

A Million Brilliant Poems Vol. 1 – Roger Stevens (Bloomsbury)

Green Glass Beads: A Collection of Poems for Girls – Jacqueline Wilson (Macmillan)

Poems for Children – ed. Michael Rosen (OXFAM)

Walking With My Iguana – ed. by Brian Moses, features John Agard, Paul Cookson, Valerie Bloom, James Carter, Wes Magee, Brian Moses and others (Hachette)

websites

Without doubt, the very best poetry resource online is the Poetry Archive, featuring poems for children and adults, from contemporary and classic poets: www.poetryarchive.org You can even buy/ download individual poems from your favourite children's poets. Plus, there are teachers' resources for KS1 and KS2. Go and have a browse!

Also well worth a visit is the fabulous Poetryzone, run by Roger Stevens: www. poetryzone.co.uk It features a wide range of interviews and poems from a whole range of contemporary poets.

The websites of the following organisations will also have poetry-related courses, resources, activities and information:

- The Poetry Society (London)

- The Poetry Library (London)

- The Centre For Literacy in Primary Education (London)

- The Story Museum (Oxford)

- Seven Stories (Newcastle)

Poetry CDs and websites

CDs

Both these CDs have a real range of voices and poems.

Use this chart as a quick reference to poems and forms of poems covered in this book which link to your classroom topic.

Topic	Form
Ancient Egyptians	Kennings, p88, Raps p85, Conversation poems p105
Ancient Greeks	Free verse p97, 'The Ancient Greeks…' p54, Raps p85
Animals	Syllabic verse, p90-91, Emotional animal rhymes p80, Rhyme practices: Pets p80, List-repetition poems p82, Counting animals p83, Alphabets p111, Kennings p88, 'Utterly Magical Animals' p69, 'How do Animals Feel?' p82, 'What Am I?' p44, Animal Warning Rhyme p66, Assonant Animals p66, Mini animal simile poems p66
Autumn/the seasons	Mid-line acrostic p110
Dinosaurs	Kennings p87
Dragons	Mid-line acrostics p110, 'If' p55, 'How To Build A Dragon' p116, 'Have You Seen My Dragon?' p68, 'Dragon Cave' p99, Free verse p99
Fables/Fairy tales	Raps p86, Conversation poems p105, 'Porky Pies!' p61, Senryus p92, 'Red & The Wolf' p106
Food	'Let's Eat' p111, Food poems p65
Memories	Free verse p95, 'Night Car Journey' p95
Minibeasts	Mid-line acrostics p110, List-repetition poems p82
Myths	Free verse p96
Ourselves	Free verse p100, Super Similes p68
Pirates	'Pirate Pete' p40, Odes p84
Rainforests	Raps p84, Acrostics p111, 'Tree' p107
Romans	Conversation poems p106
School/School trips	Free verse p97, 'This is Where' p52, 'Playgrounds' p50
Seaside/coasts	'Six ways into the ocean' p67, 'What Am I?' p44
Space	'Little Alien!' p108, Free verse p94, 'Saturn' p39, 'Zim Zam Zoom!' p38
Transport	List-repetition rhymes p82, Alphabets p111, 'Where Did We Go?' p43, 'Let's Go By' p111
Trees	Shape poems p107
Tudors	Conversation poem p106, 'Who was I?' p109
Victorians	Free verse p96, Conversation poem p105
Vikings	Mid-line Acrostics p110
Water	Free verse p105, 'The Story of Water' p60, 'Splish! Splash! Splosh!' p41, Water Web p76
Weather	'Wild, Wild Weather' p42
World War II	Free verse p97